SPEAKING IN SILENCE

ISBN 978-90-823641-1-8

www.evatasfoundation.com

SPEAKING IN SILENCE/ BUI THANH HIEU

CENSORSHIP IN VIETNAM

Translation
P. H. Thompson

EVATASFOUNDATION

Amsterdam 2015

Thanh got to work at 7:45 am and, out of habit, he proceeded to brew some tea and wipe the top of his desk. Although it was spotless, he cleaned it anyway – a daily ritual over the past ten years, ever since it had become his property.

Soon after graduating from the Public Security University eighteen years ago with a degree granted by the Counter-reactionary Department, he had been assigned to work as an intern in the Office for the Defense of Internal Political Thoughts. Five years of experience had earned him an office of his own and the position of squad leader, letting him have twenty plus agents at his command.

Thanh opened a drawer of the file cabinet to retrieve the dossier on Object B, who had been left in his charge these past two years. B was a war veteran and a poet who had once won a literary award in the province. Now over sixty years old, he had created a blog and taken to writing articles attacking the regime. His blog had attracted the attention of the Internet Propaganda Squad, of the Bureau of Culture and Communications, which had gathered his articles together and meticulously analyzed his wording, finding in it an undertone of anti-government propaganda. Subsequently, the Bureau of Culture and Communications had forwarded the file on B to Thanh's office.

Stopping such reactionary elements was a task assigned to Thanh's office, whose existence few people suspected – the Office for the Defense of Internal Political Thoughts, an integral part of Section 5 of the Department of Public Security.

Over ten years ago, the Internet had not been widespread in Vietnam, and elements like B had to put their thoughts down in longhand first and then pass their written message around, or find a photocopy shop to make handout copies of it. But these shops had been carefully watched and regularly told to be wary of possible illegal activities. The Security Office and local governments had collaborated in organizing private education sessions for owners of copy shops about how to look out for materials detrimental to national security. A hand-written text would be clear evidence of criminal wrongdoing.

At the beginning of his career, Thanh had been ordered to stake out a photocopy shop frequented by this man. One day the man had walked in and handed his poem to the proprietor to make twenty copies. Thanh then signaled to his teammates and they rushed in to arrest him when he picked up the copies still hot from the copy machine.

During those days, Thanh's job had been much simpler than it was now. With just that one case, he had achieved recognition despite only having to stay put in one location and wait for the suspect to show up with incriminating evidence in his hand.

But then the Internet had come along with a bang, and these characters no longer had to physically go anywhere to secretly pass copies of their articles around. They stayed home and used their computers to collect material and write pieces detrimental to the regime, and then sent them out over the Internet at a speed that could not be controlled like before. Checking the spread of their reactionary ideas at copy shops had become obsolete. Even the installation of a nationwide firewall only partially limited the amount of propaganda launched by these characters. In the end, the best, time-tested means was the deployment of humans, in whose hearts evil lurked.

★★★

Thanh went over the dossier containing articles written by B, supplied by courtesy of the Bureau of Culture and Communications. The batch had up to forty pages showing an increasingly strident tone, with which he even dared to blacken the Prime Minister's name. Closing the file, Thanh picked up the phone and called a subordinate.

"What are you doing?" he yelled upon hearing an electronic twittering sound at the other end. "Playing video games? Have you got nothing to do in the morning?"

"Sir, what could I do for you?" answered a voice through the earpiece. "Come over here right now," Thanh shouted. "I've got things for you to do." A young agent sporting a South Korean hairstyle stepped into the room.

"Check B's blog and search for his old articles, those with uncritical contents, and print them out for me," Thanh said. "The ones written up to 2010. And tell Dung to come in here." Skinny Dzung shuffled in.

"Get yourself down to the ward where B lives," Thanh told him. "Ask for a verification of his family background and learn where his wife's working and where his children are attending school. Tell the ward cadres to provide as much information about his family as possible. Go now!" Skinny Dzung scratched his ear.

"Could I have a letter of introduction? Those ward guys now all have their own business interests. Tell them to do something for you and very soon they all start getting restless and ready to leave, giving you sketchy details only."

"If you can't threaten the local guys, what can you do?" Thanh barked. "If I weren't here, who would get a letter for you? Just act high-handed and put all the blame on them. They're responsible for their ward and yet they let suspicious characters get online maligning and slandering the regime without being aware of it. They're only good at extorting money from restaurants and other businesses."

Even while saying so, Thanh opened a drawer of his desk and retrieved a stack of stamped letters of introduction bearing the name of his immediate superior. He wrote in Dung's name and slid it across the desk to him.

Then, pouring himself a cup of tea and taking a sip, Thanh lit a cigarette. Suddenly, he recalled that in the morning he had forgotten to tell his wife to ask his uncle for a loan to build their new house. His office had granted him a plot of land two years ago and now that his job had become stable – with him no longer having to travel as much as before – Thanh wanted to start the construction of the house so that he would have a decent place to receive his guests. The house he was living in was inherited from his parents, the front of which had been turned into a store for his wife to sell sundry goods. With New Year just around the corner, they had to stock up on goods to sell. The merchandise filled up most of the house's interior and barely any room remained for the occupants to move about, let alone for entertaining guests.

From his pocket, Thanh fished a phone, the one set aside for calling only his wife. She also possessed one only for talking with him. For security personnel – charged with the task of defending the regime, their phones were always tapped as a safeguard against potential leaks of classified information.

Thanh went out into the yard outside his office and called his wife. "Honey, were you able to get a loan from Uncle?" asked Thanh.

"He said to give him at least two more months," his wife replied. "These days, the police keep raiding his bar. Short-term tenancy for his employees is out, and without renters he's sort of hard up."

"Please tell him to try to get the money for us," said Thanh, "and let me handle that matter."

Thanh's uncle had started a karaoke bar, and he let his son run it. Sometimes, when the office had a party or when his superior needed to relax and have fun, Thanh would take them there. He wondered what the local police had against short-term tenancy. Maybe a competitor hired them to cause problems for his uncle.

Thanh went by a computer room used by his subordinates and saw Long surfing the Internet. "Long, come over to my office," he said. "I've got a big favor to ask of you."

"Yes, sir," said Long, who then stood up to follow him.

"Go to District X with this letter of introduction," said Thanh, once they both had entered his room, "and tell them to give you a list of all the hotels in Ward Y, together with relevant details of each hotel such as the number of rooms, its address, the person running the business. Tell them to put a check next to any hotels sponsored by the cadres running Ward Y for the Security Office to consider when they develop their plans." Thanh looked at the clock and saw that it was past 9 o'clock. Perhaps his superior had come in.

The day before, the heads of the departments had held a meeting with the Board of Directors. Throughout the night, they had discussed the security situation surrounding the upcoming trial of a group of reactionaries in Central Vietnam.

Several steps away from his superior's office, Thanh paused to inspect his clothes before proceeding to knock on the door.
"Come in," his superior's voice wafted through the door.

Thanh pushed it open and stepped in. His superior was sitting in his chair perusing a file. He looked up at him through a pair of clear glasses boasting an expensive Amore gold frame imported from France. "What became of V's case?" he asked. "Have you confronted him?"

"He's being watched very closely, sir," Thanh said, closing the door and bowing his head. "In a few more days, after determining his psychology, I will serve a summons on him. Yesterday, when you were meeting with the Board of Directors, the Bureau of Culture and Communications forwarded B's file to us. This morning, I set in motion the process of collecting information on him."
His superior nodded his head. Thanh sat down, rearranging the pen tray on the desk. "Sir, I have this little private matter I'd like to discuss with you," Thanh said.

His superior laid the sheaf of documents he was reading on the desk, took off his glasses, and wiped them with his handkerchief. Furrowing his brow slightly, he thought, "What is it this time?"
In his line of work, not only did he have to take care of managerial matters, but he had to pay attention to the cadres and officers working under under him as well. If his subordinates slacked for one minute, it would seriously impact their work – work on which he built his entire career.
Last year, he had completed an advanced course in ideological reinforcement at a Communist Party school. If things were to go smoothly at work, at the end of the year he could finish his Ph.D. dissertation, titled *Fighting against Organized Crime in the New Era of National Security*,

which would certainly get him the province's Vice Director of Public Security position for next year's term. With over thirty years' worth of experience in public security, he understood that he owed his success to the Organization, to the brilliant guidance of his superiors, and to the devotion and dedication of his subordinates. Security agents had to fight against criminals who, day and night, plotted against the regime, using every crafty means available. Thus, his subordinates' task was an extremely difficult one requiring a high degree of concentration.

Consequently, each agent and his family had to be guaranteed a comfortable life as well as a promising future. Only then could their dependability be secured. The superior did not immediately respond to Thanh's request, but kept looking at him thoughtfully. He took his time because he wanted his subordinates to understand that whenever they brought up some private matter, they had to consider it carefully first. This was one of his ways of creating an air of quiet authority about him. If he appeared too eager to learn about the matter and then offered to help right away, his authority would be undermined.

Seeing that Thanh seemed to be getting nervous – a sign that the desired effect had been achieved – he warmly asked, "Okay, what is it? Go on and tell me."

The superior listened while Thanh hurriedly explained the situation to him. As it turned out, it was about the bar owned by Thanh's uncle, the name of which he could not recall. He had been there twice with his colleagues from some other provinces to discuss shared projects and to strengthen personal relationships formed on mutual benefit.
A seemingly simple matter to handle, he promised Thanh that he would someday go to District X to work on the security issue regarding short-term tenancy. That trip would, by extension, help Thanh with his own family matters.

After Thanh left, the superior continued perusing the file he had been reading, then typed up a memo asking TPN, a telecommunications company, to help security agents tap the phones of the three suspects mentioned in the dossier. With that done, he took the document to the Vice Director's office to have it signed and stamped.

★★★

The young agent with the South Korean hairstyle brought a stack of papers into Thanh's office and placed it on Thanh's desk.
"Sir, here it is," he said.

Thanh leafed quickly through the stack, and feeling satisfied, he told his subordinate, "Just keep following his blog to see who he's in contact with."
"Yes, sir," said the young agent, who then left.

Thanh began to dissect B's old articles. Selecting the ones he liked, he read them carefully once more and marked them with a blue pen. Those were the articles whose contents were not too damaging, in which B had recounted the story of a resident who lost her land when the Department of Land Clearance and Acquisition wanted to set up an industrial zone to promote joint ventures. The articles provided strong evidence in the form of pictures. B had only written down the woman's experience and posted it on his blog. Thanh picked up the phone and called Tien.

Tien was the deputy squad leader, five years younger than Thanh. Tien's father was a high- ranking security cadre in the Department. Nonetheless, even with connections in high places, Tien had barely passed the high-school exit exam. As if to compensate for his lack of academic achievements, he was pretty cunning when dealing with suspects. Tien's dad regularly called Thanh to ask about his son, often suggesting that Thanh should stay close to Tien and teach him as he would his kid brother. He told Thanh to feel free to dress Tien down when necessary, since Tien only listened to harsh words. Polite speech would not penetrate his thick skull. If nothing worked, he wanted Thanh to call him so that he could make his son behave. Thanh understood that those avuncular, sugary words meant that he wanted Thanh to support and protect his son, and that, when his son did something wrong, Thanh should talk to him instead of reporting it to his superiors or documenting it.

Tien came in, his tall and big body filling the whole door frame. Carrying the gene of an ethnic group made him look different, with coarse, indelicate features. Tien's father was of the Tay race. Many years ago, the Police Department had pursued a deliberate policy of recruiting agents from ethnic minorities, whose unthinking loyalty was considered a character trait, to fight against reactionaries in the country. Saved from privation, they had sworn to follow the Revolution and the Party to the end of time. For them an enemy would forever be an enemy, no compromises or concessions ever contemplated. A number of security agents from these ethnic groups had showed strength of character and had been allowed to undergo further training and then promoted to higher positions. Tien's father was one of them.

Tien sat down, placing his iPhone 4 – the latest model – on the desk, then resting both his hands on it. On one wrist hung a gold chain, each link weighing close to two grams.

Tien poured some water for himself and drank it up. "What is it, boss? Do you want to tell me?" asked Tien. Thanh handed him a slip of paper containing the full name and address of the evicted woman mentioned in B's articles.

"Go and verify this case," he said. "After that, tell the woman involved in it to go to the village police and submit her petition. Pretend that we're helping her with it. Tell her that the powers that be found information about this case from B. Ask her to explain how she met B, where and on what date, and what they talked about. While questioning her, pretend to be reviewing her case so that she won't think that it's about B."

"God damn it! It's that woman again," swore Tien, taking the slip of paper. "She's been camping out in the flower garden in front of the

Prime Minister's palace for years, refusing to go home.

Let's dump her in the Camp for the Restoration of Human Dignity so that she can pay the penalty for being homeless. I'll interrogate her there for a few days and she'll beg to go home to her husband and children and forget all about suing the State. Getting money from squatting! Where did those squatters get that idea? Only the camp will make them change their minds."

"I'm telling you to ask her about how she met B," Thanh said, raising his voice by a notch. "I don't need you to solve the issue of evicted residents turning the Prime Minister's flower garden into their campsite. If you want to do it, I can send you to the evicted residents squad in the Office of Social Order. Over there, you can become a squad leader too."

He paused to pour some water and, sipping it, scowled at Tien.

"Damn!" Thanh went on. "You work in security but you behave as if you were chasing sellers in the market. Now go and quickly get all the information this afternoon, okay?"

Tien laughed placatingly, picked up the paper, and rose from his chair. Then, as if suddenly remembering something, he pulled out his wallet and took out some invoices.

"Boss, please sign these gasoline invoices for me," he said. "I'm broke." Thanh looked at them.

"Not even a month yet, but it's already two hundred liters," he said, his voice rising another notch. "Are you into nighttime drag races, too?"

Tien laughed appeasingly.

"They don't call it drag racing anymore," he said. "It's 'storming.' Drag racing sounds so negative. If my dad hears about it, he'll give me a severe talking-to. Just tell him I'm going 'storming' so that the old man will think I'm carrying out some important mission. He won't understand these new slang expressions." Thanh signed the invoices and handed them to Tien.

★★★

Thu was the only one left in the accounting office. She was totaling up the expenditure on tea and cigarettes and office supplies. Tien tiptoed up and quietly sat down next to her.

"Let's go to a bar tonight," he said. "There's a new one in town and a friend of mine holds shares in it. Today he's on shift. I can pick you up at 8 o'clock."

Thu tossed her hair, which was dyed to a light brown.

"No, you'll go alone because you always stay out so late. I still have a lot of work to do." Tien showed her the gasoline invoices.
"Then please take care of these for me first," he said. " I need some funds right away."

"Two hundred liters!" she yelled after a quick glance at them.

"Mrs. Hong will not approve it." Pretending to be angry, Tien slammed his fist down onto the desk.

"Let's put that old woman out to pasture for you to replace her," he said. "Old and stupid, what has she learned? One liter of gasoline can't mean exactly one liter of gasoline. Consuming one liter of gasoline requires an accompaniment of half a liter of beer or a cup of coffee. Who can drive a car forever without beer and coffee? Just tell her to try using up one hundred liters of gasoline without stopping for some liquid refreshment."

"Nonsense," Thu sneered. "I can just tell her that I've added incidentals to it and she'll approve it. You don't have to brag. Who doesn't know your dad's a big shot?"

"Having been around for years, she must understand how things work," said Tien. "I know all too well the style of those who wield power. Life is hard for a person running around in the streets like me, and so I expect sympathy, not trouble, from people sitting in air-conditioned offices."

★★★

Skinny Dzung had to search B's ward for an hour before he was able to collar the cadre in charge of the neighborhood to obtain information about B.

B's wife was an elementary teacher and his daughter would soon be graduating from high school. B had retired, and at communist cell meetings, he had often expressed ideas which strayed from the Party's point of view. His cell had frequently reprimanded him for it, and now he no longer went to those meetings.

Skinny Dzung also learned that B's family were having a conflict with some neighbors over a shared pathway. These neighbors habitually parked their motorbikes across the path, blocking the way to B's home. Many a heated exchange between the two families had thus transpired, and B had several times sent his complaint to the ward.

To obtain proof of B's handwriting, Skinny Dzung asked for a photocopy of the complaint. His mission completed, he – before going back to his office – gave the neighborhood cadre some final instructions. "This guy's a suspect my office is working on," he said. "Very soon we'll ask you to follow him closely. You should exploit the dispute between B and his neighbors and use them to keep an eye on whomever comes to see him. If you can take pictures of those contacting B, it'll help our job a lot. About the complaint over the pathway, I think your ward should organize a neighborhood meeting where B lives to discuss the issue. Choose your own guys to attend it and express the opinion that neighbors should make concessions to each other instead of fighting over matters of trifling importance and submitting complaints that will only damage their relationship. We have to do that to make B and his neighbors understand that no one will defend a reactionary like him. Let's isolate him. Once his neighbors see that the government is neglecting him, they'll treat his family with contempt. B has to learn to to behave himself."

Sensing the cadre's hesitation, Skinny Dzung went on, "Just carry out my instructions and in a few days we'll have an official meeting at the district level, with the presence of the ward cadres. At that time you'll report that you've come up with measures to deal with B. It'll help further your career, won't it?"

The cadre's face relaxed and he shook Skinny Dzung's hand heartily. "Consider it done," he said.

★★★

Long handed a list of all the hotels in Ward Y to Thanh, who, since it was time for his lunch break, put the list in his briefcase and went home. His house was not far from the office, only about three kilometers. On busy days, Thanh would have lunch in the kitchen of the office; otherwise, he would go home to eat with his wife and children. Thanh and his wife had two kids, a fourteen-year-old daughter and a ten-year-old son. His son had lunch at school, but his daughter ate at home.

With the exception of Thanh's wife, his children and their relatives only knew that he worked for the public security section in the province. Inside his house, there was a certificate hanging on the wall naming him Officer of the Year in 1997, endorsed by the Police Office for the Management and Administration of Social Order. All agents in his unit had the same sort of certificates, usually presented by a certain office so that their visitors or relatives would not ask them about their real jobs.

Thanks to his salary and job-related funds totaling over ten million *dong* a month and revenue from his wife's sundry shop, Thanh's family lived a pretty comfortable life during a time when most people had to work hard, toiling in the fields from morning till night. Among Thanh's friends, some worked in real estate and their business had prospered, enabling them to own villas and cars. But the others still had to live from hand to mouth. Besides, you never knew what misfortune might befall the *nouveau riches*, who could suddenly fall into debt and would have to hide from their creditors or the law. Compared with the penniless friends who might stay that way for the rest of their lives, Thanh's family enjoyed a stable budget and were relatively free from financial worries. His salary increased regularly with the passage of time; all his leaves of absence and holidays were perks guaranteed by the State; and free health care alone placed him and his family above so many other people.

This year, Thanh really wanted to begin the construction of the house on the piece of land his office had given him. Once it was completed, his family would move in and his wife could expand her business, buying more goods and employing a relative from the countryside as a shop assistant. Then, when his daughter started college, his son would be ready for high school. Life was full of worries.

Thanh clucked his tongue, wondering why, in a society where peace reigned, everyone was employed and enjoying a growing income, everything was normal and the economy was stable, there were many people who day and night wanted to undermine it – to upset its peaceful tempo. Normal people would continue to work and accumulate wealth. Only the reactionaries, the enemies of the Party and the State, would be scheming to overthrow the government. Those people relied on foreign capitalists to realize their political ambitions, and they would never give up their dark plots as long as those ambitions were still alive and nourished. Thanh looked at the food his wife had set on the table and saw that there were only two bowls. "Our daughter is not coming home for lunch?" he asked.

"The youth league has a field trip at noon," said his wife, "so this morning I gave her some money to buy lunch. Our daughter was honored by the school for her sense of responsibility. I think we should guide her towards an administrative career."

"Uh huh," uttered Thanh absent-mindedly, his mind preoccupied with B.

Stopping a person over sixty years old was not an easy task because of his deeply entrenched beliefs. He was not like young people, who were hot-blooded and could be incited to violence.

Thanh's office specialized in political repression, prevention of dissent, and the implementation of measures that would help educate and transform their subjects. If all measures failed to neutralize a suspect, then the suspect's file would be transferred to a security office whose agents would investigate him and instigate a criminal case.

In other words, Thanh's office was in the front line of the struggle for the defense of communist thoughts. For Thanh and his agents, success depended on how effective they were in stopping their subjects or persuading them to abandon their misguided ideas. Each time he had to transfer the file of a suspect to a security office, Thanh felt very unhappy. Even when a file was packed with solid evidence for the security office to easily indict the suspect, Thanh would still feel uneasy about it, as if he had not fulfilled his duty.

He wondered which path had led B to writing articles defaming the State. He was a war veteran, married with children (a daughter, to be precise), collecting a good pension plus allowance. He should have placidly participated in the pensioners' club, or raised poultry and planted trees, or written poems and articles contributing positively to society. What had made a person like B go down this path? Might he have had a grudge against local cadres? In numerous cases, discontent with a certain decision made by the local government caused many cadres, Party members, and war veterans to become indignant, and then they would accuse the whole machine of government of being corrupt. If their complaints were not dealt with satisfactorily, they would get agitated, and so the enemies of the regime would take advantage of that anger and would egg them on, encouraging them to irresponsibly attack the Party and the State.

The instructors at the People's Security Academy T31 were experienced, high-ranking security cadres. They regularly had to classify new-age security saboteurs and update their lectures with new information when teaching security agents. Their lectures had pointed out that due to rapid social changes, policies put forward by local governments were constantly divorced from reality, causing a small segment of the population, which had always lacked faith in the regime and helped along by the subjective judgments of local cadres and their poor grasp of reality, to become indignant.

The Party had recognized this incompatibility and had always tried to put forward timely solutions and policies. But everything took time; nothing could be achieved in a day or two. Therefore, it was the responsibility of the security cadres to take the initiative, to flexibly classify miscreants, and to design effective measures. Never before had the agent on the security front had to struggle like this, especially with his enemy aided by the Internet.

Thanh's wife scooped some rice into a bowl and placed it in front of her husband.

"Honey, go ahead and eat," she said. "What are you thinking about? You seem preoccupied. I made some calculations and saw that we only need to borrow 300 million *dong* from our uncle to build the house. We can promise to pay him back at the beginning of next year, can't we? We only need two New Years to find enough money. Just bring home whatever you can and leave the rest to me."

"Yup, sounds like a plan. By the way, in a few days, I'll remind my boss to go with me to Uncle's ward. Remember to look for a present for him, okay? He's promised to go there with me."

Thanh's wife put her bowl on the table, one hand cupping her chin. "We should ask Uncle to take care of the gift," she said, eyeing him. Thanh shook his head.

"No, it's such a trifling thing. We'll take care of it, okay? We can tell him about it later. Involving him at this point won't benefit us."

★★★

Thanh went back to his office at 2:00 pm. The air-conditioner hummed incessantly, unable to cool the air at the end of August. The rickety machine's groans prevented Thanh from concentrating on his work.

Skinny Dzung had put a report on his desk. He was the most efficient squad member. He probably had used his lunch break to write up the report. Thanh went over it a few times and then, picking up the phone, called Skinny Dzung and told him to come over.

"It was tough going down there in this heat, wasn't it?" asked Thanh, laughing. "You've done a good job. Tomorrow, go to B's wife's school and ask them about her background, her work experience, her thoughts. Then ask the principal to find an indirect way to let her know that a security agent has come and inquired about her family. The principal should also ask her to go home and tell her husband not to do something harmful to his wife and children."

"His wife's about to retire," said Skinny Dzung, shaking his head. "She's in her fifties already. And there's no reason to go to his daughter's school at this point. We should just keep him busy with the petition against his neighbors over the pathway."

Thanh tapped his pen on the desktop pensively.

"We can worry about that later," he said. "We have to meet him first and discuss his blog with him. Call Tien's older brother to see if he's back. If he is, I want to see his report now. Damn him! If we don't remind him, he'll be roaming around all day."

★★★

Tien came in and went through his papers.

"It's done," he said. "This woman was taken by C to B's house, where she asked B to write about her situation. She said that when she saw B, she gave him some documents and told him the story. B interviewed her and made a video clip of it. She said that she had to ask for help from anyone she met because the government doesn't deal with it."

Thanh took the woman's deposition from Tien, read it and put it in B's dossier. "Good!" he praised Tien. "Okay, you can go back to your office. If I need anything, I'll call you. Now I'll put it all together in a report and send it to our boss and ask his opinion on this case."

After Tien left, Thanh flicked off the AC unit, opened the window, and lit a cigarette. B's case was not that bad; there were signs that he had only just begun to take a stand against the government. Basically, his wife had a job and his daughter went to school. But the fact that C took Mrs. Nguyen to B's house for her to ask him to write a petition showed that there was a nascent network of dissenters. The National Anti-reactionary Office considered C a person of interest – to be kept under constant surveillance. He had once spent two years in jail for causing public disorder. Internal information also showed that C had contact with overseas reactionary organizations.

Now, Thanh would have to verify the relationship between C and B to determine how close they were. He would also have to write to the National Anti-reactionary Office and ask for C's file, then to the Undercover Operation Agency to ask them to keep tabs on B. Well, maybe the latter part was not necessary at this stage.

Thanh tossed the butt of his cigarette into the ashtray. He then carried B's file over to his superior's office. Opening up the file, he handed it to him.

"Sir, I have assigned an agent the task of collecting information on B," he said. "First, I'm planning to select some of his articles which will provide a legal basis to summon him to appear before us. Making him acknowledge the existence of his blog will be the first step. Therefore, when talking to him I won't mention the articles highly critical of the government right away. Here are the ones I have chosen to entice him to come and see us. He'll be able to justify writing them, but that's how we'll make him admit to the ownership of the blog. Once that's happened, we'll bring him back to discuss the critical ones."

Thanh's superior nodded and flipped through the dossier. "Will we ask him to come here or somewhere else?" he asked.
"I'm planning to ask him to go to the district police office," Thanh answered, "to make it look as if the district is receptive to ideas from the people. He'll be less suspicious."

Again, Thanh's superior nodded, then took an already-stamped letter of introduction, signed it, and gave it to Thanh.

★★★

B had received a summons from the district police the night before. It stated that the police needed to discuss the contents of Mrs. Nguyen's petition with him.

Mrs. Nguyen had lost her land and received just a pittance as compensation, and so she felt that she had been wronged. Her garden had been part of a piece of residential property for generations, even the jackfruit tree – everyone knew that its trunk was big enough for you to wrap your arms around, which meant that it had been around for decades. But the acquisition officials blatantly said that she had lived on her land illegally because she didn't have the little red book as proof of ownership. Back when the State was providing little red books to land owners, she had, several times, submitted an application for one, but because she didn't grease the palms of the village committee members, they had dragged their feet over it for several years until the Committee of Land Clearance and Acquisition wanted to free up some land for roads, and claiming that, without the red book to prove otherwise, her land had been illegally inhabited. So they had evicted her and based compensation for the loss of her land on the price of the crops that could have been grown there.

Going over the whole incident in his mind, B concluded that probably the village committee and the Committee of Land Clearance and Acquisition had been in cahoots. They said that it was cropland and had given her a small sum for it, but they perhaps had later filed it as residential land in order to collect a much bigger sum as compensation. Obviously, the whole land area bordering on Mrs. Nguyen's had been settled and farmed for a hundred years, complete with an ancient five-room house with a tiled roof. It was not a piece of silted-up land along a river bank to be called ownerless.

A sense of joy stirred inside B, a veteran of many battles from north to south. He found that he could still do something for humankind, for some unfortunate people who had been mistreated.

From the day he stopped working and collected his retirement certificate, he had gotten more time to look around him and recognized that there was room for improvement in many areas in his society – areas that were in fact truly deplorable. Before he retired, he used to come home after spending eight hours in his office, read a newspaper, watch television, and then go to bed.

At work, in the newspapers, and on television, he had learned that life went on smoothly, with an occasional flood here and a blocked road there – things which were not to make light of, but not to be severely critical of either. Floods were natural disasters, but the government could have made a better job of preparing for them and limiting their impact. As for roads that got blocked, there were only that many streets, but people from everywhere kept coming in, so it was a natural consequence. However, ever since he retired, he had recognized that there were other kinds of disasters in people's daily lives.

Before, B used to leave home early, so he had not known that his neighbors during the day had turned the pathway into a parking place for their motorbikes. Irresponsible and selfish, they occupied that whole shared space, regardless of what would happen if there was a fire or an emergency. The pathway was intended for use by everyone; it did not belong to them alone.

Other folks in the neighborhood had expressed their opinions and he had authored a complaint letter and submitted it to the committee. But despite the fact that it had been submitted again and again, no official had dealt with it. People said that nowadays government officials only dealt with things that would earn them good money; there was simply no profit in moving the motorbikes to make way for some folks.

Several times, when B had gone to the ward office to turn in one more copy of the complaint, he saw that the ward cadres would expedite any paperwork that could generate cash for them, like notarizing some document that enabled them to collect a fee of ten thousand *dong*. They would notarize one form after another, and there were so many people standing in line with their forms in their hands. Plus, the fee had to be handed over before the notarization.

B had debated with himself whether he should enclose some cash with the complaint letter as an incentive for the ward cadres to help solve the issue of the pathway.

★★★

"Damn this corrupt society! Damn this corrupt regime!"
The stinging words and familiar voice of the old man selling lottery tickets on sidewalks came into his mind. The old man and B had been childhood friends. B had joined the military and his friend had become a worker in a mechanical plant.

When the military changed its policy, B had been allowed to retire early. His friend had also retired early, but it was because his strength had been sapped; and instead of a pension, he had been given a lump sum. His factory had lost much of its business and had to turn its land over to the private sector. Factory workers who had not reached retirement age would be forced to retire if they lost their strength, and the standard lump sum would be twenty or thirty million *dong*, to be deposited in a bank. Unfortunately, annual inflation would eat into the amount and shrink it considerably. He had been withdrawing money daily to buy lottery tickets and exhausted his savings in half a year. But thanks to the experience he had gained in buying lottery tickets, he had taken up a new occupation, which was the sale of lottery tickets.

One day, B had asked the lottery ticket seller why he kept calling it a corrupt regime. "I curse a regime that forces you to retire when it has used up your strength," said the lottery ticket seller. "May the regime be damned for it! I have served it all my life, so I deserve, as you do, a pension that will be inflation-adjusted every year. At my plant, they kicked us out in order to sell the land to the capitalists for them to build a business district. We didn't need the twenty or thirty million *dong* they dished out to us. The money loses its value every day. After six months, it was all gone, so I no longer could buy lottery tickets to live in hope. A corrupt regime. A deceitful regime. Robbers."

Mr. B decided to give his friend some advice.

"Don't be so quick-tempered," said B. "This is only temporary. Inflation has many causes, including the international situation. The State couldn't have connived at dishing out a sum to you and then making inflation rise. A temporary policy is adopted to solve a temporary situation. The State and our society aren't as morally bankrupt as you think."

The lottery ticket seller just got angrier.

"I curse the whole society. Damn them all! They let an old man with poor eyesight sell lottery tickets on a street corner, getting a small percentage for each ticket sold. Rain or shine, I have to be here, but then just the other day some street urchins tricked me into selling my tickets for a fake two-hundred-thousand *dong* note. Tell me if this isn't a morally bankrupt society, cheating even a lottery ticket seller on a street corner. Society's morals have gone down the drain, while the State has produced a police force as enormous as the Mongol armies back then. As talented as our police are, they still can't catch the counterfeiters. Let me ask you this. Which is harder, printing fake money or printing propaganda leaflets? Try printing propaganda leaflets. It takes them just a few minutes to come and catch you. I have this friend of mine who used to write silly stuff mocking them. When he got to a copy shop, they had been lying in ambush for him. How talented they are! Fake money printing machines must be more sophisticated than the ones producing lottery tickets, but they cannot find them. A morally bankrupt society!"

Finding it hard to calm his friend's anger, B had bought a few lottery tickets from him. Now, he found his friend's words, like the story about counterfeit money and propaganda leaflets, worth pondering over.

★★★

Mrs. Nguyen had for years been suing the village committee; now you could find copies of her petition at every level, from the Central Committee down to the village committee, in all offices and departments, and yet no one had taken a look at it. She then had asked B to write an article about it and post it on the Internet. It had only been a few days and some government officials already asked to meet with him. How strange! B had only suddenly had those thoughts, but he believed in himself as a former senior cultural cadre in the military – a party member, a war veteran, a soldier who had held a gun plunging into battlefields. All his life, he had been an unselfish person serving the common good. The government had to respect his words.

Full of hope, the next morning he got up earlier than usual and put on his plain military uniform bearing no insignia, save for the national emblem, which he pinned to the soft visored military cap. He also carefully copied the video clip he had made when he interviewed Mrs. Nguyen, together with pictures of the petition and related documents to a USB drive and took it with him.

Leaving the house, he found the neighbors' motorbikes blocking the way, and his annoyance came back. He had half a mind to yell at them, but he was afraid that it could lead to a heated exchange which would make him miss his appointment. Swallowing his anger, his moved the motorbikes out of the way and went down the pathway.

★★★

Thanh was discussing a few things with a district police cadre.

"Yes, you can just make the introductions and ask about the

issue as we have planned," he said. "Then I'll ask him some additional questions. Okay, our man should be here any moment now.

Our undercover agents say that B has left his house and is on his way here. We should get ready, and please let me record this meeting." When B arrived, it took him a long while to find the parking lot, which was in the back of the district police office. At first, the guards told him to take his motorbike out to the flower garden. He protested, saying that he had been invited here. He didn't come to ask the police a favor, so he didn't understand why he had to take his motorbike to the flower garden. They relented and directed him to the backyard. A clerk waited for him to park his bike, then he led him upstairs to a room where there were three cadres waiting for him, one of them in uniform and the other two in civilian clothes. The one in uniform wore the rank insignia of a major. He stood up and shook B's hand and made the introductions.

"Greetings!" said the major. "Here are the two cadres handling Mrs. Nguyen's petition. This gentleman is a municipal administrator and this gentleman—" He pointed at Thanh. "—is a city police cadre. Please have a seat. Would you like a drink? Tea is ready, but if you prefer coffee, it will be brought in."

Thanh took his time observing B. His face had harsh features, indicating a conservative person, hard to be persuaded. B accepted a cup of tea. The three cadres also drank tea and appeared friendly, but in fact, they were all trying to figure him out.

"Mr. B, we have learned about Mrs. Nguyen's situation through your blog," said the major, opening a file. "As you know, it is our responsibility to handle complaints and petitions from local residents. Since Mrs. Nguyen's petition is posted online, it doesn't have her signature. We have printed a hard copy of it, but it's not an original copy. Please certify that this is an exact copy of her petition. Then, allow us to forward it to an office authorized by the committee to handle such petitions. They will handle it over there because we don't have the authority to deal with civilian matters. We work in public security, but we can help people bring their complaints and petitions to the right place so that they won't waste their time."

When the major paused, Thanh handed B the printout of Mrs. Nguyen's petition.

"Please take a look at the letter and make sure that it's the right one," Thanh said. "Your language is as concise as a lawyer's. Perhaps you know a lot about law. The petition and the supporting documents are all there, nothing's missing. I don't know what they do over there in the committee office, but they let their residents send their petitions everywhere. It's their job to receive them and deal with them properly. Anyway, just consider us an intermediary for these petitions, like you. Since you are here, please verify her letter and we will keep a record of it. Then I'll send the letter over to the committee. Once they've responded to it, I'll let you know, hopefully in a week. Is that okay with you?"

Thanh paused for a moment, then went on, "So, Mrs. Nguyen wants to be compensated for her loss of three hundred square meters of gardening land. Is that right?"

B's sense of justice was immediately aroused. He hurriedly cut in.

"Not just those three hundred square meters of gardening land. You have to include forty square meters of the walkway leading to the garden. That walkway is also part of her land."
Thanh pretended to look at it again.

"Yes, there's also forty square meters of the walkway," he remarked in a seemingly naive voice. "Why didn't you tell her to write it as three hundred forty square meters?"

B fell into Thanh's trap, believing that they were truly interested in Mrs. Nguyen's petition and would try to force the issue on her behalf. He thought that his blog and his words had had some effect on the government. At least, he was able to produce some positive results, unlike Mrs. Nguyen who had been knocking on numerous doors for nothing. He felt a little proud of himself and at the same time pitied these police officers who did not seem to have a firm grasp of the issue.

"It's three hundred square meters of gardening land, so Mrs. Nguyen should be compensated for her loss of fruit trees. In addition, it's three hundred forty square meters of land in general. So, she should be compensated for her loss of fruit trees on three hundred square meters of farmland as well as for her loss of a total land area of three hundred forty square meters. It's that clear-cut."

The three government officials mumbled something and nodded, pretending that they understood B's explanation.

"Yes, that's right," said Thanh. "It's got to be separated like that. Here, I've found the paragraph about the forty square meters. It's right below."

Thanh turned and said to the man in civilian clothes sitting next to him.

"Record that on this day, the district police office received the petition from Mr. B who has been authorized by Mrs. Nguyen to submit the letter on her behalf."

Then he turned his head and looked at B.

"You are authorized to submit the letter only, correct?" asked Thanh. "I don't think you're authorized to get involved in the issue of compensation."

"Yes, I'm only submitting the petition on her behalf," answered B contentedly. "You can talk with her about the issue of money. I don't want to be involved in it."

Thanh nodded his head in agreement. Then he turned to the other person and dictated an official report of the meeting.
"It should go like this: It is recorded that we have received the petition authored by this citizen on this date at the police office of District X. We, the following people, holding such and such a position, have received Mrs. Nguyen's petition regarding a certain issue as follows..."

Thanh cleared his throat and went on, "While sorting out the backlog of petitions according to the decree issued by the Prime Minister on such and such a date, the district police discovered on a blog titled..." Thanh asked B, "What's its title?"

"The Voice of the Homeland," replied B.

"The blog called 'The Voice of the Homeland'," dictated Thanh.

Suddenly, he turned to B.

"'The Voice of the Homeland' is written as one word, without diacritics, or is it written in the regular way?" he asked.

"As one word, without diacritics," said B.

"So is it a Facebook or Multiply or BlogSpot account or something else altogether?" asked Thanh.

"A BlogSpot account," said B.

"Did you write that down?" Thanh asked his colleague.

His colleague nodded. Thanh continued, "On 'thevoiceofthehomeland.blogspot.com,' owned by Mr. Tran Van B, a blogger, there is some information about Mrs. Nguyen's petition regarding a certain land issue. Mrs. Nguyen was born in such and such a year and resides in this village of that province. We helped print out, from Mr. B's site, Mrs. Nguyen's petition, which consists of three pages. There are four pages of supporting documents and a picture of the piece of land originally inhabited by Mrs. Nguyen. Mr. Tran Van B, the owner of the website titled 'thevoiceofthehomeland.blogspot.com,' verifies that these documents were printed in full from his site. Nothing is missing or added or taken out. Mr. Tran Van B suggests that an office tasked with handling residents' complaints and petitions should review Mrs. Nguyen's case and solve the issue according to the law in a timely manner. The report is concluded on such and such a date."

Thanh went through the report and then handed it to B.

"Please read it over and sign it. We've completed the proper procedure, as dictated by the law, for receiving this petition from you. That's all there is to it. Please also sign in the margin of Mrs. Nguyen's letter. And if you have any other suggestions, please write them down at the bottom of the letter, together with your name as the person authorized to submit the petition."

B felt very satisfied. He looked the report over, for the sake of appearances. Then he signed the report and the petition.

The district cadre filled out a two-part receipt for the acceptance of the petition. While doing it, he asked B for his phone number, explaining that he wanted to call him the moment he got an answer to Mrs. Nguyen's petition.

B told him his phone number and took the receipt. Having concluded their business, they all stood up and jubilantly shook each other's hands. B felt that they were truly amiable. At least in this bureaucratic machine there still existed some people who were devoted to the masses and dedicated to their work. B felt that he had done something beneficial for such a powerless person as Mrs. Nguyen. Perhaps she would be overjoyed when she saw this receipt.

He retrieved his bike and rode home with a light heart. He did not know that those documents would never go to any committee; they would be inserted in a dossier carrying his name, safely stored in a clandestine security office, among a myriad of other security offices across the country, created solely to defend the ideology and the Party. Very few people and government cadres were aware of their existence.

The cadres who remained in the room were also joyous. They laughed heartily and patted themselves on the back for a job well done. Thanh put B's file in his briefcase, thanked the district cadre, and went with his colleague back to their office.

When seeing his cheerful face, Thanh's superior asked, "How did it go?"

"Very well, sir," replied Thanh happily. "Our man acknowledged that he owns a website called 'thevoiceofthehomeland.' I'll question him again in a few days. I have a report here, together with his signature. As for the recording of the meeting, I'll copy it to a USB drive later."

★★★

B left his house early in the morning to attend a demonstration staged by some people protesting against a neighboring country's act of aggression. It happened that B's country had a couple of small groups of islands within its own territorial waters, and quite unexpectedly this neighboring country now declared the islands to be their own. Then they sent their navy to occupy the islands, killed some of his country's sailors, put up buildings, and explored the area for natural resources. Fishermen from his country were shot at and their boats destroyed when going fishing around those islands. Some died at sea while others were made to pay a fine because they had illegally entered this neighboring country's waters.

The tragic irony was that B's government and the government of that country had a special, ironclad brotherly relationship. Therefore, his government only dared call those incidents a misunderstanding about who had sovereignty over the islands. His government suggested that the people should not act recklessly, and asked them to have faith in the Party's resilient diplomacy towards that neighboring country because both countries were led by a similar type of party and these two parties had to foster close relations in order to survive under pressure from global politics. The survival issue was considered the State's top priority, and they termed it political stability. From this viewpoint, any demonstrations against the neighboring country's aggression could cause disharmony between the two parties and would lead to political instability, which would then undermine their one-party State. That was the reason why his government treated protesters as plotters trying to bring down the current regime. The security and secret service machine had been created for the defense of the Party, and their agents would follow protesters closely and find ways to break up any rally.

When B left his house, there were two men in their early thirties waiting for him across the street. They were ready to follow B on their motorbikes.

First, B rode his bike to a certain location to pick up a friend. Then when B and his friend – both aged and with gray hair – were about to mount the motorbike, one of the men following B got out his iPhone and snapped a series of photos of the two old men.

There were just about ten people gathering at the demonstration. The protesters had just unrolled their slogans when a police car with a loudspeaker screwed to its roof arrived on the scene. A voice boomed out ordering the crowd to disperse because they were disrupting public order. The authoritative voice had barely ended when a score of tall and muscular guys wearing red arm bands rushed the demonstrators and twisted their arms behind them and pushed them onto a waiting bus and took them away. The two old men trembled as they stood rooted to the spot, witnessing the protest being stamped on ruthlessly. Three guys grabbed a woman's arms and dragged her away in front of B. He quickly blocked their way and tried to take hold of the woman.

"Who are you? Why are you dragging a woman so brutally?" shouted B.

The three guys pushed him aside forcefully, but he jumped right back in to stop them. Immediately, four more guys, also wearing red arm bands, sprinted toward him. One guy twisted his arms behind him while another guy put his hands round his throat to prevent him from calling out loud. Then they pushed him toward a bus, where two more muscular guys helped pull him onto it. The bus careened out of the city center and soon pulled to a halt in front of a small prison camp in the suburbs. It was called 'The Facility for the Restoration of Human Dignity.' Here, the police held beggars and prostitutes.

★★★

The demonstrators were kept in a spacious yard surrounded by a high wall topped by barbed wire. Cops armed with AK-47s and electric batons and clubs stood guard at both the camp entrance and the exit.

"Good Heavens!" exclaimed a demonstrator. "We held a protest march to express our love for the country and they took us to the Facility for the Restoration of Human Dignity. Does it mean that we have lost our dignity?"

Another protester looked around and saw a row of small rooms with beds inside. "Maybe these are the living quarters reserved for the cadres?" he wondered.

Among the demonstrators, there was a man about forty years old, looking as if he had gone through a lot. He spent some time looking around.

"This is a prison camp," he concluded. "Look at the high wall with barbed wire on top, the water tank with iron bars across. The windows have iron bars. The doors can only be locked on the outside, no locks to be seen on the inside. So, it means these are prison cells. For cadres? They are for prisoners."

While the demonstrators were still puzzling out why they had been arrested and for what crime, at the main entrance the cars carrying investigators from various branches and offices continued to roll in. One car was from the religious security branch, one from the social security and public order office, one from the cultural security section, and still another one from the anti-reactionary security department. The protesters were then classified and selected for each office to interrogate. High school and college students were questioned by the cultural security investigator. The Catholic protesters were interviewed by the religious security officer. Some other protesters were brought before the investigator from the social security and public order office. Those who were classified as special elements were interrogated by the anti-reactionary security cadre.

But the most notorious elements were questioned by the security and investigation specialist. These elements were special cases; they were already being followed and in all probability would be receiving jail terms. Those belonging to this category had gone through the verification process initiated by the security branches and their individual files had been forwarded to the security and investigation office, which was the sole security organ having the power to arrest a suspect, recommend putting the suspect on trial, and initiate a criminal prosecution. The security and investigation office would document every activity of the suspect and would patiently build their case and, when the investigators deemed it necessary, take them to court.

★★★

When the young cop led B into the interrogation room, Thanh had already been sitting there. "I heard that you were here," greeted Thanh with a broad smile, "so I had to come right over to work with you. The other offices don't know your personality, so things wouldn't go well. Please have a seat."

Thanh brought out some deposition forms, to which B objected. "What crime have I committed that requires my deposition?"

"You and your friends gathered and disrupted public order, a violation of Article 38 CP issued by the government," said Thanh. "Here it specifies that when there is an assembly of over five people in public places, you have to obtain a permit from the government. Did you apply for a permit? You didn't, did you? So obviously, this is a violation. A person well versed in the letter of the law like you should know better."

B stood firm.

"We didn't just gather. We protested against the aggressors. We sided with our compatriots who got killed at sea. At my age, I don't have any free time to go out and cause public disturbances."

"Demonstrations must follow the law, but the State doesn't have a law for them yet," said Thanh. "The National Assembly is considering introducing such a law. Under the present circumstances, you violate the law when you demonstrate. In addition, the Security Office has received a dispatch from the Bureau of Culture and Communications, informing us that the telecommunications company that you subscribe to has discovered on your blog 'thevoiceofthehomeland' articles attacking the government and inciting people to demonstrate and cause public disturbances, discrediting the Party and the State, and eroding the public's trust in the government."

"If you do wrong, the public will lose faith in you," interjected B. "Just do right, then who can speak ill of you?"

Thanh put the forms down and gravely looked B in the eye.

"The law has a provision for citizens to lodge complaints and expose corruption," he said pointedly. "If something isn't right, the public can write to specialized offices. It's unscrupulous to write articles and post them on the Internet. It's indicative of an abuse of freedom and democracy, harming the interest of the Organization, of the State. Pursuant to Article 258 of the criminal law code, you can be made to stand trial. I suggest that you should be serious and truthfully answer all the questions asked by the Security and Investigation Office."

Thanh paused for a moment and then asked harshly, "Tell me your full name."

B didn't answer him. He was simmering with rage. So the guy who had received Mrs. Nguyen's petition at the district police office turned out to be a member of the secret service. They had deceived him from the beginning. With everything seeming to have gone south, he no longer cared and decided to let them say whatever they wanted to say. Thus, he remained silent.

Presently, Thanh smirked as he had just worked out a strategy for luring B into his trap. He poured himself some water and took a sip. "If you don't tell us about yourself and your family, we will take your fingerprints and your picture and send them out to various places for the purpose of verifying your background. Meanwhile, we have the right to hold you because we don't know your family, and because you refuse to cooperate fully with us. I would advise you to let me take your deposition. Don't be so obstinate. Your name's Nguyen Van B, is that right?"

Thanh then softened his tone and pretended to jot something down. "No, it's not Nguyen Van B. It's Tran Van B," B corrected him. Thanh wrote the name down and continued with the deposition, asking B innocuous questions about his family members.

B began to feel nervous. At first, he thought he had not broken any law. But the inquiries about his family members – where his wife worked, where his daughter went to school, and what grade she was in – made him suspicious.

"I'm responsible for my own actions. Why do I have to talk about my wife and daughter?" he asked, raising his voice.

Thanh chuckled threateningly.

"The deposition-discovery procedure requires the disclosure of family background, which means information about your siblings, parents, wife and children. That's why it's called a background check. If you don't want us to ask those questions, then don't do anything that forces us to ask them. We'd be crazy to randomly grab people from the streets and drag them in here for a deposition. We don't have time to waste and to look for trouble needlessly. If you don't let us depose you, we have other ways to obtain all the information. Do it willingly, and we can soon wrap it up and you can go home."

Eventually, B gave in and started talking about his wife and daughter, giving Thanh their names, information about his wife's workplace, and his daughter's school. Thanh copied everything down. "Your daughter's such a good student," said Thanh sneeringly. "Which university entrance exams is she studying for?"

In dumb disbelief, B realized that they had carried out a thorough check on his family. What was their intention? Why had they done it? He had heard a lot about what happened to authors and artists who had been critical of the regime, about how their wives and children had suffered at work and at school. His daughter was about to sit for a few college entrance exams. Would they dare to intervene and find a way to lower her scores? Clenching his teeth, B swore that he would fight to the death if they did that to his daughter. But where could he get evidence against them? What if his daughter had not done well on the exams?

B pursed his mouth and frowned thoughtfully.

"You aren't thinking clearly," added Thanh, seeming to have read B's mind. "Your daughter's about to take some exams. Keep doing this and the government can't afford to leave you alone. Let me ask you this. If you're held like this, would your daughter be worried? Of course, she would. When worried, how could she concentrate on her studies? I care about you, and that's why I'm telling you this from the bottom of my heart.

Think about that."

Thanh then asked B about the article posted on 'thevoiceofthehomeland' on the day of the demonstration. He asked B where he had written it, when he had written it, whether he had used a desktop computer or a laptop. Thanh kept delving into all the small details as if he was trying to obtain enough evidence to convict him of a serious offense. He also wanted to know what had motivated him to write that article, and what he knew about the ways and policies of the Party and the State regarding foreign relations and the issue of sovereignty. It was getting dark when Thanh handed the deposition to B.

"Read it over to make sure that everything's correct," he said, "and sign it to acknowledge the clause which reads, 'I declare that the information provided above is true and I accept full responsibility for any false statements.'"

B held the six-page deposition and read it carefully and picked up a pen to sign his acknowledgement.
Thanh took back the pages and stood up.

"Please wait here a moment," he said. "The district police office has something to tell you. As for us, we'll soon have another meeting. When you receive our summons, please come on time."

When Thanh exited, two cops in uniform came in. "Mr. Tran Van B," they loudly intoned. "Please listen to our decision to impose a penalty on you for disturbing the peace."

B was taken aback, unable to fully comprehend what was going on. They read out the prepared statement so fast he only caught a few words here and there, but enough to get the gist of it.
The district police concluded that B had violated this article and that item of the criminal law code. However, they decided to just issue an administrative warning this time. The statement had been read out to the party involved at 19 hours on such and such a date, certified by a police representative from the ward where Tran Van B resided.
They carried on with the statement for a while, and then told him to go home. B had to drag himself to the gate. The day had been filled with so

many happenings. It was also the first time he had had a tense encounter with cops. He felt listless. He went out into the street and took a bus home. On seeing him, his wife started to cry.

"Dear oh dear!" she cried. "What did you do? Why did they arrest you? This afternoon, our neighborhood leader came and told me that you had been arrested for disrupting public order at the city center. I was sick with worry! From that moment until now, I haven't been able to think. Our daughter and I kept waiting for some news without knowing where it would come from.

Some people around here heard it at the ward office that you had joined an overseas reactionary group and received money from them to incite people to protest, harming national security, and then the reactionaries would use the opportunity to overthrow the government. Oh my! Why do you do such a foolish thing at your age? Don't you know that every neighbor is a police informer? Whatever you do, they know. Our neighbors have informed on you. They also say that you've written many reactionary articles, criticizing the regime. In your free time, you should just go to the pensioners' club in the ward to play chess, and, when you're in the mood, write poetry with some other old men there. Why do you have to write silly stuff on the Internet and cause suffering for your wife and child? If you don't love yourself, at least you should love us."
Hearing his wife say many strange things, B got upset.

"Who told you that I should go to the pensioner's club and play chess and write poetry?" he demanded angrily.

Mrs. B pointed at the door.

"When they heard the neighborhood leader say that you had been arrested, some seniors showed up and told me to advise you to stop doing foolish things. They said that if you want to write poetry and rhymes, you can go to the pensioners' club, and if you have any concerns, you can write to the local Party members and the ward government. They also said that if you write on the Internet, the reactionaries will take advantage of you. They will hail you as a hero and give you the mistaken belief that it is a good thing, and you will be tricked into writing more articles."

B turned away, waving her protests aside.

"Stop it, and let me be. It's been a long day and I'm tired."

Skipping dinner, B went into his room and lay down. With an arm resting on his forehead, he thought for a long while before falling asleep. At midnight, he woke up and went to get some water. As he walked past his daughter's room, he saw a light on. He glanced in and saw her still studying. Tiptoeing to the outer room, he quietly poured himself a drink of water, then went back to bed. But he could not sleep. They now had invaded even his home and influenced his wife to stop him. This was just the beginning. He wondered what would happen next. He pictured the horrors of the cultural revolution that he had heard about: family members separated from each other, your grown children forced to work in remote mountain areas and their residency permits revoked, and many other such stories. Exhausted after a stressful day, B finally fell into a deep sleep.

★★★

Having been waiting for that moment, his wife sat up and covered him up with a blanket. She didn't sleep; she lay still and observed him. She had wanted to say something before he fell asleep, but held it back because it would just make him angry again. Earlier, he had gotten upset, so she had not dared to go on. Some retirees from the pensioners' club, who were former Party members, had told her that the Public Security Office were reviewing B's criminal act and that he might get thrown into jail. But, if his family could reason with him now, maybe he would repent of his ways in time, thus avoiding a jail sentence. Everything, they had said, would depend on her husband's remorseful attitude.

B's wife suddenly recalled that recently her neighbors had been acting strangely. The other day, she had taken a motorbike taxi driven by Long. When collecting the fare, Long had said that her family had no lack of money because her husband now worked for foreign countries.

At that moment she had thought that he might be jokingly equating her husband's retirement with employment in a foreign company. Now she realized that those around her had known about what her husband had been doing. No longer friendly and neighborly, they had been whispering about her family behind her back and looking at her inquisitively. When she had gone to to collect B's pension at an office and was leaving, she had overheard a snatch of conversation.

"What is a regime? A regime means the pension account from which you draw your money monthly. If the regime is gone, then the pension account will be gone too, like what happened in Russia. Over there, you can't collect your pension any more. As long as you still receive your pension, you have to defend the regime. Which countries in the world are free from corruption? But sooner or later it will be stamped out. Just don't receive money from somewhere else and act against the regime."

She had thought that those folks were talking about some matters in faraway countries such as Russia and America. Now she understood that they had been gossiping about her husband.

"My dear husband!" she thought to herself. "Why are you so foolish? Speaking out against the regime hasn't taken you anywhere, and now your neighbors have become resentful of you as if you were acting against them. They are the same neighbors who for decades have been willing to face any hardship with you, and now suddenly they've become your enemies. How can we survive this?"

★★★

Thanh went to B's ward to meet with the chairman of the ward, the Party secretary of the ward, and the police chief of the ward. All three of them had been waiting for him in the People's Committee's conference room, and they all shook Thanh's hand enthusiastically.

In the room there were the two indispensable slogans, one reading 'Chairman... Lives Forever in Our Lives and Work' and the other saying 'Long Live the Glorious Communist Party.' In the middle of the room was a bust of the Leader. The layout of the room was aimed at making all Communist Party members attending a meeting feel that they had to devote all their energies to serving the regime, and pledge their loyalty to the Communist Party, which was in sole command of the entire nation. The Leader of the Party whose bust was sitting there would hear everything they said and discussed, and would judge whether they were working unstintingly for the Communist Party or not. Nothing could escape his saintly eyes: the Leader knew everything. He could detect signs of negligence or lack of devotion. He would use his moral compass and his thoughts to make his disciples discover any person who was not devoted or was straying from the fold. That person would then be disciplined, criticized, demoted, or hauled off to court to receive a sentence.

The chairman of the ward poured some water and the Party secretary of the ward brought out a pen and paper and set them on the table.

"Let me give you an update," said the Party secretary. "We have come up with a strategy for dealing with B: we are using the local residents. The pressure of public opinion will help us admonish B for what he's doing and educate him about how he should behave. The ward police have also begun to keep tabs on his every move. Please drink some water. I know how tired you all are."

The Party secretary looked at the police chief. The police chief understood him and picked up the narrative from the Party secretary.

"The moment you informed us," he said, "we immediately established a network of informers using mostly local residents, and had our man surrounded. We've been watching all the comings and goings of B's visitors. We have involved the neighborhood police officer in this case and now we'll ask him to work overtime in order to provide professional training for all the various informer networks to ensure that the information we receive is accurate and useful. Here is an initial report on B's every movement."

The police chief handed a sheaf of papers to Thanh. Thanh smiled and thanked him and the ward police for their thoroughness and hard work.

"Because B lives in a neighborhood under your management," he said, "you've had to work so hard. Still, we need you to be more determined, actively attacking him from various directions. The aim we're proposing here is to make him abandon his anti-government activities. Our assessment of the situation is that B is acting on his own, without the support of any organization. In our dealings with this type, we have to be creative and flexible. Arresting him and taking him to court will not work to our advantage at this point, especially because he used to be a Party member and a government official. If we put him on trial now, we wouldn't have time to prepare public opinion. Secondly, Western countries would criticize us for suppressing freedom of speech. We suggest that you guys use *strong measures*, but don't let our man have any evidence against us or any opportunity to create a ruckus. It's best to give it the appearance of a conflict between neighbors. If necessary, let them come to blows, but any injuries must be determined to be under ten percent. After a few brawls like that, our man's spirits will be so low he will abandon his criminal activities."

The ward cadres looked at each other as if to send a telepathic message. Then, all three of them nodded their heads. Thanh stood up and shook hands with each of them.

"If you guys need our support, please call us," he added. "Or even better, keep us posted on your plan so that we can provide timely support."

★★★

Sitting in a beer bar, Thanh waited for a friend working in construction to come and talk about the building of Thanh's house. They had been friends since high school but had not seen each other for quite a while. A couple of years back, Thanh had met him by chance in front of the city police department and learned that he had been involved in some shady deal, buying materials with padded bills issued by some ghost company. In a state of panic, he had told Thanh about his precarious financial position – the project coming to fruition, only to be suspended, pending a police investigation; thus bankruptcy was imminent while he still had to make interest payments on his loans.

Thanks to Thanh's intervention, the police had concluded that his friend had committed no violations because he had not known that he had struck a deal with a ghost company; he had only received materials that came with the bills. With Thanh's help, the issue of buying materials from one company while getting the bills from another had become buying materials and receiving the bills from one single company, and so became a crime no longer.

Having gotten out of that dangerous situation, Thanh's friend had become indebted to Thanh. That New Year's Day, he visited Thanh and offered him a bottle of wine and fifty million *dong*. Thanh declined the money, saying that friends always helped each other out. Thanh's friend replied that the sum of money was for Thanh to buy gifts for the investigators involved: because they had overlooked your wrongdoing, you would have to treat them right. He said he was not repaying Thanh for what he had done for him. To repay Thanh, he promised to send his construction workers over whenever Thanh wanted to build a house, at no cost to Thanh, with nothing to worry about.

"Okay," Thanh had said. "I'll arrange for you to meet with them and give them the money, because you might have other dealings with them in the future. If I brought your money to them, they might think that I'd taken some of it for myself. It wouldn't look good for both you and me."

The following week, at a restaurant specializing in wild game meats, Thanh arranged for his friend to meet with the economic crime investigators.

It had been two years since. The other day, Thanh had called him and told him that he was planning to build a house. His friend was eager to meet, but Thanh had been too busy with B to do so. He had found some free time today.

Dealing with B was a task assigned to Thanh's office. But Thanh had passed it onto the ward guys. They would be responsible for it, and Thanh had been careful to put nothing in writing and give them no clear orders. These planned brawls, if carried out too enthusiastically, would cause a stink. Passing it onto the ward guys was by far the best option, and he would be free. Also, it would look like a neighborhood dispute, without any interference from security agents.

Thanh's friend came, asked a few polite questions about his family, and started talking about the construction of the house.
"You choose a date and leave the rest to me," the friend said. "I'll take care of it, from A to Z. I'll take some materials from the other construction projects to save some money. I'll assign three main workers to it and hire some apprentices. I already have all the scaffolds and formworks and other construction equipment, no need to rent any of them. Agreed? Leave it to me; nothing for you to worry about."

The construction of the house having been agreed on, Thanh's friend hurriedly stood up and said goodbye. Thanh stayed, sipping his beer and ordering some sour pork sausages. Rarely had he had all this free time like this, a luxury to enjoy while knowing that you had made great strides in dealing with important matters.

Suddenly remembering that Tien's house was nearby, Thanh took out his phone to call him and ask him to join. When Tien showed up, Thanh ordered some more beer and food.

"Have a drink," Thanh said, sliding a mug of beer in front of Tien. "I just called on the off-chance that you were home."
Tien took a swig of beer and unwrapped a sour pork sausage.

"I'd just got home," he said. "Our big boss told me to go find Tu's house. She is an accountant in Quang's company. Maybe this time we'll arrest him for tax evasion. We've found several pieces of evidence to put in his file."

"Did you find her house?" asked Thanh.

"Yes. She's renting an apartment," said Tien, "and she's two months pregnant. Perhaps I'll ask her to come and see us in a few more days. It seems she's a cousin of Quang's. I've found out that they're from the same village and Quang brought her up here from the countryside to work for him."

Thanh became pensive. Quang was a Catholic. He had gone to law school and then opened an investment consulting firm. A few years ago, he had founded an association of Catholic entrepreneurs at his church, and Thanh's superiors had determined that Quang was planning to establish a political organization. At the same time, he had been writing articles for the BBC adopting a critical tone toward the State. As this was an act of shaping public opinion, Quang showed that he had the ability to engage in politics. Quang was trying to gather momentum before entering politics as an accomplished entrepreneur, a knowledgeable lawyer, and a morally upright parishioner. If they did not nip his scheme in the bud, later it would be very difficult, since his influence over society would be immense. To defend the regime, they had to uncover the harmful seeds at the very beginning in order to annihilate them, preventing them from growing. But if they arrested him for contributing to foreign media outlets, it would just make him famous. That was why Thanh's superiors were now planning to put him away for tax evasion, thus neutralizing his reactionary activities. They would also succeed in destroying his credibility and leaving no legal loopholes for people to criticize the government for arresting political dissidents.

Quang's case had been in the works for the past three years. Perhaps his accountant would prove to be his Achilles' heel. The psychology of a young woman pregnant with her first child could not be as stable as that of other young women. Her maternal love was bound to affect her deeply when she was brought before the law. Thanh fingered the rim of his beer mug and turned it around, sighing.

"In the coming months our job will become harder," he said. "Our country will join the United Nations Human Rights Council, and maybe the Trans-Pacific Partnership. Under these circumstances, the way we deal with the political dissenters must be different than before. We'll have to limit trials for those arrested on charges of spreading anti-government propaganda, which means we'll have to employ stronger warning measures without leaving any evidence behind for them to find us out and make accusations on social networking sites."

"Just ram into their bikes and give them a severe beating and they will remember it for life," grunted Tien.

Thanh looked into Tien's eyes and saw in there a fiery rage. Tien was the most quick-tempered among his subordinates. Thanh read them all very well, which enabled him to hand out proper assignments.

Tien was mean, getting into fistfights and gambling throughout his high school years. Although he was given priority over other applicants for being an offspring of some VIP in the field, he had been rejected by the Public Security University because of his extremely poor grades. Tien's father then had decided to enroll him in a mid-level police academy.

Tien was able to perform many tasks too hard for the others to do. Thanks to his appearance, Tien could blend in easily with people in the streets to gather information. He was also useful when needed to play the role of a member of the criminal underworld.

"Go to B's ward tomorrow," said Thanh, nodding his head. "Those ward guys and you will collaborate in dealing with B. Tell them to choose a family for you to stay with, and tell everyone that you're their nephew from the countryside. Stay there for a week and get it done. They've already come up with a plan, so just go there and discuss your role in it."

★★★

Throughout the week, Mrs. B had found that Mrs. Chinh – her next-door neighbor – twice daily brought out her honeycomb coal stove and started it right next to a side wall of her house, beneath a window. Mrs. Chinh used old bike tires to kindle a fire, which produced clouds of thick smoke. Mrs. B had gently asked her to bring it elsewhere. Mrs. Chinh had glowered at her.

"We share this pathway," she said. "Your house faces it, so you'll have to put up with it. If you can't, then move farther down the alley. In this life, everything has its price. I'm poor, so I have to use a coal stove, I've got no money to pay for a gas stove like you, understand?"
B complained to the neighborhood leader about Mrs. Chinh's stove polluting the air.

"It is said that neighbors should help each other out," said the neighborhood leader. "Mrs. Chinh lives in difficult circumstances because her husband sacrificed himself in the war. She lives by herself and she has to depend on an income from the State. She is very thrifty, so as a neighbor, you should sympathize with her and find a way to help her. If for such a trifling matter you bring each other before the local government, you will only cause a lot of hostility between the two families."

The neighborhood leader perhaps did talk to Mrs. Chinh, so this morning when Mrs. B went outside, she found that Mrs. Chinh now used firewood instead of bike tires to build a fire. The smoke no longer smelled of rubber, but it was still suffocating nonetheless. Mrs. Chinh was fanning the fire when she saw Mrs. B stepping out of her house.

"Damn the reactionaries," said Mrs. Chinh out loud. "They use every means to harm honest people. If they ever held power, they would strangle the people. What kind of democracy, what kind of freedom are they talking about? Every day they even trample on the little food and the little water poor people got. Just don't talk about big things. Mean neighbors, how could they help the whole country?"

Inside his home, B heard it all. He stepped outside and confronted Mrs. Chinh.

"Your cooking affects other people's health. You have to stop. And don't use that sarcastic voice."

It seemed that Mrs. Chinh had been waiting for this moment. She stood up and, wagging a finger at him, delivered a diatribe.

"Hey, let me tell you this, scumbag. Don't you play games with me. Suing and complaining? Who doesn't want to live in peace? All the houses here get exposed to the smoke and they don't say anything. I've had to take my wardrobe apart for the firewood. No more smoke from the burning rubber, and yet you aren't satisfied. Now, you demand something else."

"It was a broken wardrobe someone had dumped in the garbage dump at the head of the alley," Mrs. B cut in. "You brought it home and chopped it up and now use it as firewood. You're saying it as if it were your own wardrobe. And as a matter of fact, we don't want you to start your stove here."

"What can you do about it?" Mrs. Chinh howled. "Scumbags! Reactionaries! You must be thrown into jail. You must be taken into the jungle to produce timber. You're well-fed, but you sue the government and pry into the lives of the little people. Now I'll use whatever I have to start my stove. I'll use even my pubic hair to see how you'll react to its smell."

B completely lost it. He darted into his house and darted out again with a mug of water in his hand. Then he went straight to Mrs. Chinh's coal stove and upended the mug over the flames. The stove gave out a long hissing sound and then the fire went out. Mrs. Chinh rushed B, scratching him. "Scumbag! You've destroyed a citizen's property. I'll teach you a lesson."

B tried to pry open her grip and while they were pushing back and forth, a tall, big young man opened the door of the house owned by Dung and his wife Thanh to take a look.

"Help! Help! This guy's trying to kill me," Mrs. Chinh yelled.

The young man agilely approached B and clamped one hand around his throat while gripping his side with the other hand. It was a professional hand squeezing his floating ribs, and B heard a soft crack and felt a sharp pain before he crumpled to the ground. As the whole world turned dark before his eyes, he vaguely heard his wife shouting for help.

★★★

B was hospitalized and got a rib brace. Everyday, his wife came to take care of him. On the third day, the ward police came to see him after they had received a complaint from Mrs. B.

"Are you feeling better, Mr. B? Can you work with us? If you aren't feeling well, we can always come back. At least, we've got the results from your doctor."

B nodded and said, "I can answer your questions. Go ahead."

The cop who had come with the ward police chief sat down next to B, opened his briefcase, and brought out a pen and some paper. Then he put the paper on the briefcase.

"Please state your name, age, address, and occupation," he said.

"You are the ward cadres," said B, feeling annoyed, "so you already know my address, name, and age. Why do you make me give you all this information when I'm still in pain like this?"

"This is a matter of principle," the ward police chief said. "Even though we know it, we still have to ask you to make sure that it's the right person. If you don't feel up to it, we can wait until you are better." Hearing those words, the cop who was writing down B's statement pretended to put the paper away, as if wanting to end the interview. B had no choice but to ask them to get on with it and answered a bunch of boring questions about his family background, stating all the known facts such as his name, his birthday, his address, his job, his wife and daughter, his siblings, his parents, et cetera, et cetera.

The cops did not hurry to get to the main business. They meticulously asked how old his brothers were, how old his younger siblings were, where they lived, where they worked. As for his deceased parents, they also wanted to know when they had died, why they had died, whether they had died from disease or from old age. An account of how he had been injured suddenly became an account of his family.

B patiently answered all the questions about his family, which took up the best part of an hour. From time to time, the cop doing the recording would again ask him about someone in his family. B felt exhausted. Mrs. B brought him a bottle of water and put a straw into it. B grimaced when sipping water through the straw while the ward police chief and the cop looked on icily.

They seemed annoyed because the interview had been interrupted.

When B had finished drinking, the note-taking cop asked, "When the incident happened, what were you doing inside the house?"

"I was reading a newspaper," said B.

"Do you often stay home and read a newspaper around that time or go somewhere else?" asked the cop.

"I often stay home and read a newspaper at that hour. That's what I often do in the morning," answered B.

"Some neighbors say that at that hour you usually take a walk in the park," the ward police chief cut in, "and then go drink coffee with some guys exercising with you in the park until ten. Why did you stay home that morning?"

B wanted to sit up, but any movement caused him a sharp pain. The doctor had told him to lie still, having broken ribs requiring it.

"I don't go to the park every day," protested B. "It's not a daily exercise routine." "Please tell us why it isn't a daily exercise routine," demanded the note-taking cop.

"I can't take a walk on rainy days, on cold days, and when I don't feel well. On those days I can't go," said B.

"That morning it wasn't rainy and it wasn't cold either," the cop sneered. "So it must mean you weren't feeling well, because you didn't go out. But you still had plenty of stamina to pick a fight with your neighbor. Please answer our questions truthfully to help us get to the bottom of this incident. So on that day, why did you stay home at that hour?"

B wanted to scream but he felt completely drained of energy.

"I was a victim," said B, clenching his teeth. "Are you taking down a victim's statements or interrogating a criminal? It's my house, so I can come and go anytime I want."

"Hey, Mr. B," the ward police chief said with a grim face. "You write petitions and articles. I thought you understood the law. Right now, you're only a party who got injured in the fracas. We haven't been able to determine who the culprit is in this case. We are investigating it objectively. We haven't come to any conclusion. Once we have clarified certain things, we will conclude who the culprit is. Right now everyone involved in this case is being asked the same questions."

The note-taking cop tapped the end of the pen against his palm while gleefully listening to the heated exchange between B and the ward police chief.

"I see that you're very hot-tempered, Mr. B," said the cop doing the recording. "You're working with government officials who follow legal procedures and you still lose your cool like this. I wonder how you'll behave in other situations."

The cop's remark pushed B over the edge.

"What other situations?" he snarled. "Are you implying that I was the one who had provoked them into a fight? Are you guys trying to frame me for it? Remember that I'm the person who was harmed and beaten up, but you are treating me as the sole culprit."

"We've already explained to you," said the note-taking cop with a sneer. "We have to get enough information to determine the cause, the motive, and the act. They are the links in the chain. In order to determine the cause, we have to ask about the time, the relationships between the involved parties, and other things. If it were that easy, everyone would go into this investigation business without having to go to school for a number of years, and then train professionally for a few more years, before getting to hold a pen and take down statements. Harming an innocent person is a serious matter. Therefore, our law pays a lot of attention to the investigation process. We even have a State ordinance which says that harming innocent people must be avoided."

"So you said that on that day you were home," the ward police chief chimed in, "and were writing some articles to post on your own website. You can talk about what you were writing. That would be a logical explanation. So what were you writing at that hour?"

B felt that they were springing a trap when urging him to talk about his writings on the Internet. "I wasn't writing anything," said B. "I was reading a newspaper."

"Usually you go out," said the cop, "but that day you stayed home and read newspapers. Obviously, there are many days when you don't go out at that hour for various reasons. It is raining. There is a cold wind. Your friends are coming to visit you. And so on and so forth. So why did you stay home on that day?"

B thought that they were still trying to maneuver him into talking about his articles. They wanted to verify that he had been writing an article at that hour so that they could pursue that line of questioning. If he answered that he had been writing, they would ask what he had been writing, and demand to see his laptop and look at that article. They would then be able to get hold of both his laptop password and his website password.

"On that day I was sick, so I stayed home," said B.

He said that he had been sick because if he said that he had been well, they would accuse him of intentionally staying home to cause trouble, of having planned to pick a fight with his neighbor.

The note-taking cop wrote down B's statement. In fact, the cop was not a member of the ward police even though that was how he had been introduced to B. His name was Cuong, from the security and investigation office of the city police department. Cuong was an experienced investigator who quickly had a firm grasp of the psychology of any suspect. Before coming in to depose B, he had worked with the ward police about the direction of the deposition. During their discussion, he had explored all the possible responses from B. The questions asked by the ward police chief were part of a plan to distract the suspect. B would get suspicious when asked about his articles, and so he would try to be evasive about it. And from a psychological standpoint, there had to be a hidden reason. They only needed to wait for the right moment to make B give the right answer and then they could conclude the investigation as planned. They would explain in B's file that his being sick on that day was the reason why a man could get injured when fighting with a woman. If he had been well, the opposite outcome would have been expected.

Based on numerous court cases, even if it was just a mild fracas, a sick or drunken person could fall and die from a concussion. The unfortunate incident could be deemed unintentional when one of the persons involved was an old woman or a young child who was not strong enough to inflict an injury on any other party. The injury was unexpected, no one willing it to happen.

But he would worry about that later, as he needed to resume the interrogation. Having scored an initial victory, Cuong focused on the next few questions.

"So, as you have stated, a young man clamped one hand around your throat and broke your ribs with the other hand. Did anyone witness the incident?" asked Cuong.

" My wife and Mrs. Chinh," said B.

"Your wife's a family member," said Cuong, "so her words are not conclusive. As for Mrs. Chinh, who was involved in the fight with you, she claimed that the young man was just trying to separate the two of you without causing any injury to you. We'd written it down, but we also thought that her claim wasn't conclusive. To confirm anything, we need to gather more factual information. So please tell us about the relationship between you and that young man. Do you know each other? Is there any resentment between the two of you?"

"I don't know him. And there's no resentment of any kind between us," said B. Cuong then adopted a sincere voice as if wanting to help him.

"That young man is a nephew of Mr. Dung and Mrs. Hanh's. Is there any private vendetta between you and their family? They probably took this opportunity to attack you."

54

Dung and Hanh were government officials, and there had been no disagreement of any kind between the two families. When meeting in the alleyway, they often nodded in acknowledgement, but never talked with each other. Moreover, Dung and Hanh had never paid much attention to the goings-on in the neighborhood.

"Their family and I have had no disagreements."

"So, when the young man saw you argue with Mrs. Chinh," said Cuong, "he just jumped in and grabbed your throat and broke your ribs. Did he say anything, maybe cursing you for hitting an old woman?"
B's eyebrows came together in concentration.

"No," said B, "he just came up to me and grabbed my throat and broke my ribs. He didn't say a word."

"Did you say anything?" asked Cuong.

"It was so sudden there was no time to say anything. Also, my throat was squeezed, how could I say anything?"

"After being attacked, did you fall down?"

"Yes, I did."
"When falling down, you were in so much pain you didn't know anything, not even aware of being taken to the hospital."

"Yes, I fell down and felt a sharp pain in my ribs, and then I fainted."

Almost done with the interview, Cuong wrote a few sentences on the bottom of the last page.

"Last question," said Cuong, looking up. "Are you completely certain that you don't know or have any feud with the young man who attacked you, or with Dung and Hanh, his uncle and aunt?"
B nodded his head. The deposition was over and it was read back to him. B asked his wife to fetch him his glasses so that he could look it over. Then he signed his name. The police officers said goodbye to him.

★★★

After having left the hospital for half a month, B still had not heard from the government about the incident. He fired off a letter to the court, and another one to the district's procuratorate. He had to wait forty five days before he received a notice from the court. The notice said that his complaint was not backed up by evidence solid enough to merit a lawsuit. The district's procuratorate gave him a clearer answer. They said that there had been no attacker, no culprit, and therefore, they could not start a lawsuit. Enclosed with their letter was the conclusions of the investigation conducted by the police. B read the following excerpt:

"This incident was caused by a small dispute in the neighborhood activities. B's floating ribs were broken because he got involved in a fight when he was sick. When he pushed Mrs. Chinh, Mr. B was quite unsteady on his feet and therefore slipped and fell on top the stove and broke his ribs. Mr. B's statement that he had been attacked by Nguyen M. Tien, a nephew of Dung and Hanh's (Dung and Hanh were Mr. B's neighbors), has no foundation. There were no witnesses.

We were also able to verify that Tien was a morally upright person, having never fought with anyone before. This fact matches Mr. B's statement that he did not know Tien and had never been in conflict with him, and neither had he ever been in conflict with Dung and Hanh. The main cause leading to Mr. Tran Van B having his ribs broken was his being ill when getting into a fight with Mrs. Chinh. Mrs. Nguyen Thi Chinh is the wife of a deceased soldier, living by herself. She is 68 years old and weighs 47 kilos. She is 1m52 high and has a thin build, and is feeble in her old age. On the other hand, Mr. B is a younger person, weighing 65 kilos. His statement that Mrs. Chinh had pushed him and made him fall is groundless.

"We thus suggest giving a warning to all parties involved in the fight. At the same time, we suggest that the local government should educate their residents and urge them to obey the rules which govern public order and security and avoid causing internal conflicts in the life of the community ..."

B froze and his face became purple with rage. He couldn't believe that people could be that treacherous. He sat pondering how to put together another complaint and pursue the matter further.

For several days, B just sat drinking his wine. He only brought out his medicated wine jar every now and then as a therapy for arthritis. He would also drink a few shots of the wine on the occasion of a festival or an anniversary or Tết. The jar was kept in a corner of the kitchen where few people would notice it. Now, he had brought it into the living room, and at regular intervals he would tilt it and fill the shot glass. He felt that his complaint would go nowhere. Those members of the court would read his file and, finding only that much information, would not be able to fathom out his case. They would only read the investigation report and the conclusions submitted by the cops; they would just look at the cops' statements and their interpretations.

They were bound to trust their own people, because they all worked for the same government. They would not trust a commoner like him.

★★★

In recent days, a heavy atmosphere enveloped the whole house, making everything seem surreal to Mrs. B, and she became absent-minded. Knowing that her husband was full of bitter resentment, she didn't dare talk with him and stayed as silent as a shadow. She and her husband had gotten married late, and the pregnancy had also come late. After her daughter was born, her doctor had told her that she should not think of having another child, for the second pregnancy would be very dangerous for both mother and baby.

Mrs. B hoped that the recent fracas would not adversely affect her daughter, who in just one month would take a college entrance exam. Mrs. B now even took better care of the ancestors' altar. Every morning, she lit some incense sticks and prayed to her ancestors for help protecting her family and keeping them safe as in previous years.

She reminisced about a peaceful time, when they had been poor but safe and happy. She and her husband had gone to work and collected their salaries in the form of food stamps. During those days, everyone led a frugal existence, no filthy rich people like you saw around you nowadays. Back then, those enjoying wealth engaged in shady business. They had money, but they would not dare to flaunt it. But today, the well-heeled were all government officials and communist leaders; they had both money and power. They flaunted their wealth and engaged in decadent activities openly. They themselves had caused society to become increasingly morally bankrupt.

She loved her husband for being upright and enduring the immorality of his time. She loved her petite and pure daughter who very soon would have to navigate her way around a society full of paradoxes, nonsense, and temptations. She wished that her husband had been less upright, ignoring injustices and moving with the times. Then, maybe their life would be better. Where the whole society was going, if you criticized it, it would be like banging your head against a brick wall. You would be doing harm to your family first.

She vaguely understood that the fracas in which her husband had been beaten up was not an accident. She wondered whether he knew that. Several times she had overheard people say that every reactionary would be punished one way or another. They had spoken about that at the sticky rice stall this morning and at the sundry shop this afternoon. She knew that they had said those words for her benefit.

Mrs. B also did not dare talk with her husband about the teachers' meeting she had attended at school recently. At the meeting, they had indirectly talked about enemy forces who were taking advantage of freedom of speech and of the Internet to disseminate anti-government propaganda. The school had reminded that all the teachers had to uphold the ways and policies of the Party and the State in their classes. If at home a family member of a teacher had made the mistake of committing those kinds of infractions mentioned above, it was that teacher's responsibility to remind the family member to stop making that same mistake. Otherwise, for those students and parents who knew that their teacher had a spouse who was a reactionary fighting against the regime, would they still trust that teacher and would the parents continue to let their children absorb knowledge from that teacher? The headmistress also added that she had received some recommendations from parents for such a case. But the school decided that they had only been the recommendations of a few individuals; therefore, at this meeting she just wanted to remind her teachers of the potential danger of it all so that they could proactively deal with such family issues.

Now, she knew why her neighbors had increasingly looked at them uncomfortably, and why they had parked their bikes on the shared pathway in front of her house. She and her husband had suffered silently and bitten their tongues. And suddenly, there was Mrs. Chinh starting her stove beneath her window. Then there was the nephew of Dung and Hanh's coming here out of nowhere. After he had beaten B, Dung and Hanh never offered any explanation. Instead, they told Mrs. B and her husband that because of them, their nephew who had been staying with them while looking for a job had to go back to the countryside. They also said that Mr. B, accustomed to attacking the government, was now wrongheadedly making allegations against their nephew and suing him.

★★★

This morning, two of B's friends came to visit. They were loyal fans of his blog. When they left his house, two young, thuggish-faced males had used their phones to take pictures of them and the license plates of their motorbikes. One of B's friends confronted them.

"Do we know you? Why are you taking our pictures ?" he asked.

One of the thugs answered in a provoking voice, "I can't take pictures of these houses? Damn these troublemaking reactionaries!"

B hurried out to intervene and, pushing his friends toward their bikes, he forced them to go home. The thugs looked at him with open contempt. Observing their aggressive attitude, he realized that they had the same mannerisms as Tien, the nephew of Dung and Hanh's, who had beaten him. Now, he understood why he had been beaten, why his neighbors had picked a fight with his family, and why his complaint had not been solved, and why the police had written up those conclusions in their investigation into the fight. He knew that if he tried to follow through with the complaint, he would be indicted for calumny. He turned cold when recognizing that the law no longer existed in this country. Now, the authorities dictated the law and could arbitrarily conclude that he was right or wrong. The legal system created by the State had become a tool for protecting the authorities. That was its ultimate purpose.

★★★

Someone's voice came through the door. "Are you home, Mr. and Mrs. B?" B recognized that it was Mrs. Lan, a fellow teacher of his wife's. She had come with her husband, carrying a bag of fruits.

"Are you feeling better?" they asked warmly, stepping into the house. "How depressing! In our old age, our bones become very fragile. How did this happen? We vaguely heard about it the other day. We haven't been able to find the time to visit you until today. We brought you some fruits."

Mrs. B took the bag of fruits and set it on the table, then she went to brew some tea for their guests.

Mrs. Lan was both a teacher and a union member and had been a fellow teacher at Mrs. B's school for decades. They were as close as sisters. Both their families often visited each other; therefore, their husbands had also become close. Mrs. Lan's husband, Mr. Tu, made a business of fixing motorbikes at home, so their family had a pretty comfortable life. Mr. Tu was fond of reading books and newspapers and listening to the news, so he got along well with B. The two of them could chat all day long without getting bored. Repairing motorbikes was interesting because you had the opportunity to talk with your customers, mostly to make them less restless. There were all kinds of customers with different kinds of experience; therefore, Mr. Tu knew more about life than B.

The pot of tea ready, Mrs. B brought it over to the table and set it down. "It's been a long while since you last came over," she said. "My husband's got a lot on his mind to tell you about. Please stay and have lunch with us and enjoy some wine with him."

Since they were close friends, Mr. Tu nodded his acceptance. The two women immediately set out on a grocery shopping trip, letting the two men stay home and share confidences.

After hearing B recount the brawl and what B guessed were the reasons behind it, Mr. Tu thought for a moment.

"Well, we have figured out the reasons," he calmly said. "But the truth is we can't do anything about it. The law's in their hands, so they can distort the facts at will. You're still fortunate enough to be alive. In these chaotic times, a gentleman has no alternative but to save himself first. It's already a good thing that we're still able to resist an urge to go with the flow and become as corrupt as they are."

B shook his head bitterly.

"I never thought they could be this bad! I never thought they would resort to all those dirty tricks when dealing with their own people. In my articles, I'm only talking about what's really happening. I'm not distorting anything or slandering anyone."

Mr. Tu slapped his hand against his thigh.

"There!" he cut in. "It's because you tell the truth. They aren't happy and they can't invoke the law and put you on trial. They resort to the law of the jungle, the law of the underworld, the law of the mafia, you see?

If you tell lies about the regime, they can apply the law and throw you in jail. Don't think you'll always be in the right. Maybe they're reading your articles. They may force someone mentioned in your articles to say that what you've written is not right. For example, you write about this man who lost his land. If they want to, they can give it back to that person and persuade him to accuse you of making things up. So you'll have to go to court and receive a sentence. Who can defend you then?"

It was time for him to take his medications. B went to the head of his bed and brought out a nylon bag and took out a few tablets and popped them into his mouth. Mr. Tu quickly handed him a glass of water to help him swallow his tablets. He then offered to help B lie down on his bed, but B gestured for him to stop.

"I'm feeling much better, but I still need to take some calcium. My body isn't in pain anymore. Let 's go back to the table and drink some more tea."

The two old men sat looking at each other, each following his own train of thought. "They may also try to harm our family," Mr. Tu said while ruffling his gray hair. "As you know, they even harm their own comrades, injecting them with poison; they may accidently pull the trigger as they go hunting; and the children of their enemies get sent to work in the mountains. Instead of being promoted, you may get trampled all over. That happens all the time; they'll stop at nothing."

Suddenly, Mr. Tu lowered his voice.

"My wife says that at her school," he whispered, "there's a rumor that some parents have written to the headmistress claiming that there are teachers whose husbands are reactionaries who slander the regime, and they want the school to investigate and decide whether such a teacher should continue teaching when her husband regularly breaks the law. These parents demand to know how she could be a role model for her students. They say they need to feel safe enough to keep sending their kids to school while they're working day and night to help the country to stabilize and develop."

Mr. Tu then gave B a pat on the shoulder.

"There! Why do you think those parents know about your family? There must be some snitch among them, but if we ask them, they'll explain that by chance a friend sent them an article and when they read it, they felt outraged because it was just a gross distortion of the facts, and, after some research, they discovered that the author of the article is Mr. Tran Van B, the husband of a teacher who's teaching at this school."

Mr. Tu paused and sighed.

"Their spies are present everywhere," he continued. "They call it 'the battlefront of the people's safety and security.' Every citizen is a public security agent. You can put up with this, but what about your wife? It must be painful for her to see you beaten up like this. Then, when she goes to her school, she hears people complain about you, whispering bad things about you. Maybe she hasn't dared tell you about it."

Filled with despair, B buried his head in his hands.

"No, she hasn't told me anything. How could they be that evil? Have they lost their humanity? Do their leaders support them in all of this?" Mr. Tu waved a hand in front of B's face as if he was trying to rouse him from a bad dream.

"If their leaders hadn't ordered them to do it, they wouldn't have dared," said Mr. Tu. "And these aren't just verbal orders. Look at what they declare in the newspapers: 'We have to take the initiative and be creative in the task of preventing the suspected elements from spreading their anti-government propaganda.' Each nation is supposed to have its own national legal system, its laws and rules. Everything must be done according to law. Then why do they urge their citizens to be creative? If law enforcement officers are allowed to create their own enforcement measures, then it must mean that the law doesn't exist anymore. If it's all about creativity, then it means they have the right to bend the law at will. Which means they can ignore the law completely. I must say, your complaint will go nowhere. It's no use pursuing it."

"How could they be that evil?" howled B. "I will expose the true face of their system."

"You expose the true face of their system?" said Mr. Tu, laughing bitterly. "Do you think they will let you do it? Do you think beating you up and firing Mrs. B will be all? What about your daughter?"

At this point, Mr. Tu raised his voice and put his cup of tea down forcefully.

"They may sideswipe her bike and make her fall. They may send two guys to follow your daughter, then on a deserted stretch of a road, they pretend to tease her and push her. Falling from a bike may have unpredictable consequences. I've been fixing bikes for years, including bikes involved in accidents. Like people often say, human life is so fragile. Because of our long friendship, I've always treated her as though she were my own daughter. I hope you will think about her."

"I ... I ... I will kill anyone who harms my daughter," howled B anew.

He then stood up as if he wanted to go somewhere, but Mr. Tu held him back and gave him some more advice.

"Maybe I'm talking too much. Please don't be mad at me. But even if you could kill them, your daughter might already have been harmed. Nowadays, there's no shortage of people for hire to do that kind of thing, and they don't lack money. They only lack heroes and martyrs. Nowadays, if a traffic cop chases a truck to demand some bribe money and falls off his bike and dies, he'll be hailed a hero, a martyr. Then, they will also honor him for his heroism in the newspapers and on television. Our people have always had compassion for heroes who had to sacrifice themselves in a war. The feeling has become part of their subconscious. Having a half-a-million strong police force, they must hope that one of them will die such a silly death every ten years or so, so that they can hail him as a hero and win public sympathy in the process. They must hope for it much more than we do."

The two women were back from the marketplace and the two men did not carry on their unfinished conversation. The women went into the kitchen to prepare some dishes as the two gray-haired men stayed lost in thought. After a while they switched on the television to watch sports, but they could not concentrate after such a depressing conversation.

★★★

Thanh picked up the phone and received an oral report from a subordinate.

"Sir, the old man and his daughter are going somewhere. I saw her wheeling the bike out of the house and the old man locking the door."

"Just follow them and give them a fright on the way back," ordered Thanh.

★★★

It was said that crab meat soup would help your injuries to heal faster. These days, crabs were rare because they could no longer survive in paddy fields full of chemicals used in pesticides and fertilizers. Yesterday, Mrs. B was able to buy some of them. When her husband and their daughter went to the hospital this morning, for the doctor to check his injured ribs, she told them to go to the market on the way back and buy some water mimosa as another ingredient besides the taros she had bought before, for her pot of crab meat soup. At noon, when she was back from work, she would prepare the soup for the whole family.

When the two of them left the market, B stood waiting for his daughter to retrieve her bike from the parking lot. Suddenly, he noticed two young males sitting on a motorbike wearing caps instead of helmets. They were fixing him with an icy stare over their surgical masks. B found it odd that they had no helmets, and yet they were trying to protect themselves from air pollution. He took another look at them and discovered that they were the same thugs who had loitered in front of his house, aggressively taking pictures of his visitors the other day. B realized that they had been following him, which made him wonder why, since he had only gone to the hospital and had not handed out leaflets or done anything illegal. A little while later, the mystery was solved. When they were approaching a turn in the road, his daughter flipped on the turn signal and carefully looked behind her. Seeing that it was clear, she started to turn when the thugs on their black motorbike zoomed by and the one riding pillion gave the front wheel of his daughter's bike a kick, startling her and sending her bike reeling for one scary moment. B and his daughter almost fell off their bike.

"Fuck you!" the thugs cursed after braking sharply. "Driving without keeping your eyes on the road? You will get killed making a turn carelessly like that."

B's daughter was about to get off her bike to argue with them, but B stopped her and looked deeply into the thugs' eyes. The one riding pillion pulled out his phone and took a picture of B and his daughter standing in a daze in the middle of the road. He knew what they were doing. Inside his head, he again could hear Mr. Tu's voice warning him that they would not spare even his daughter. B pursed his mouth, shook his head, and laughed bitterly.

★★★

'Soldiers from hell' was the official title held by these demons. When peace reigned supreme and the light of justice and charity shone bright all over the country, the soldiers from hell had no place to live, so they had to hide themselves in the dark regions. When the country was plunged into chaos, lawlessness, immorality, greed, and perfidy spread like wildfire and the soldiers from hell reappeared and thrived. They invaded the hearts of normal people and manipulated them.

They were commanded by cruel wizards wielding magical powers. These wizards ordered their soldiers from hell to exploit the people and confiscate their wealth, and to heap revenge on those who dared to defy their masters – the wizards. The wizards of today were miracle workers. They only needed to sign a memo, nod or shake their heads, and the very next day, they would have a mansion and billions of *dong* in their pockets. Thanks to their magical powers, they were able to build vast armies made up of soldiers from hell to occupy every street and every alley, ruthlessly stamping on anyone who dared to expose the secret of their dark powers.

★★★

B stood in front of the ancestors' altar, letting his nebulous thoughts blend with wisps of smoke from the burning incense. He found himself completely lethargic, as if someone had slowly pulled all the tendons from his bones. He left the altar to go to the sofa and flung himself down on it. There was a knock on the door. It turned out that it was the neighborhood cops. They came to hand B a summons from the district police demanding him to come to see them because someone by the name of Tien complained that B had made false claims about him. The neighborhood cops said that he had to obey the order; if not they would have to frogmarch him there. After a bad coughing fit, B took the summons and went up the alley to catch a motorbike taxi.

At the district office, he learned that there was a letter from Nguyen M Tien detailing the fight between Mr. B and Mrs. Chinh, claiming that Tien only tried to separate the two of them, but that Mr. B still attempted to get a hold of Mrs. Chinh, and when Mrs. Chinh stepped aside, Mr. B had slipped and fallen down and injured himself. Tien complained that B had distorted the facts and falsely claimed that Tien had beaten him. Tien was vindicated after the police department had looked at the case seriously and investigated B's claims thoroughly and concluded that Mr. B had made false charges against Tien. Now Tien wanted Mr. B to compensate him for the damage to his honor and for the time he had lost in the legal offices.

The police officer holding the rank of lieutenant colonel slid Tien's complaint letter in front of B.

"Please read the complaint. If you have anything to say about it, then here is a pen and paper. We have to pursue all legal disputes. First, we will listen to both sides. Then we will judge the charges on their own merits. If it's not serious, we will treat it as a civil case, to be settled out of court. Otherwise, we must take it to court."

"I'm the one who was beaten," said B, a bewildered expression on his face after reading Tien's complaint. "He's the culprit. What should I ask of him now?"

"We have verified how you were injured," the district police officer said coldly. "We have reviewed the evidence and witness issues. Both the Procuratorate and the Court have agreed with the investigation office that you fell down when fighting with Mrs. Chinh. There is no witness who can testify that you were beaten. But since you charged that Tien had beaten you in your signed testimony here, without any proof to back it up, you'll have to write a letter asking to withdraw your charges. Still, it'll be up to the defendant to pursue it or not. If he does, you'll then be asked to appear before a court of law."

The district police officer paused and looked at B threateningly.

You should remember that the law requires proof," he said sharply. "It can't be arbitrary. If you have proof, show it."

Then his voice became low and conspiratorial.

"Tien was staying there to look for a job," he sweet-talked. "Because of you, he had to go back to the countryside, still jobless. Maybe he won't let you off the hook that easily. Now, write up a letter requesting that all charges against Tien are dropped and at the same time offering him your apologies. We will arrange to meet with him and try to work out a reconciliation between the two of you. If you both don't insist on pressing charges, then maybe the case can be wrapped up soon. There! Look at his complaint, then write down your decision as to whether you want to press ahead or be reconciled with Tien. Just sit here and write it. I need to go and take care of something else, but I'll be right back."

The lieutenant colonel went to the door and called for a young cop.

"Just see to it that he has everything he needs. Bring him a pot of tea too."

The young cop brought in a pot of tea and set it on the table, then went out into the hall to play with his phone. B sat alone in front of a blank sheet of paper. He hesitated, pondering over the matter. After a while, he picked up the pen and wrote his request that all charges against Tien be dropped. The lieutenant colonel came back, picked up B's note, read it, and nodded his agreement.

"We should try to live in peace with everyone, as the old saying goes. With this note, we can easily persuade Tien to drop his charges too. Why should you keep suing each other? There are so many other things that must be done. Now you can go home."

★★★

Thanh read B's note and saw that toward the end of the letter, B stated that there had been a misperception on his part due to his old age and his poor eyesight, and that he hoped Tien and the police department would forgive him. Thanh nodded and put the note in his briefcase, and then stood up and shook the lieutenant colonel's hand.

"Thanh you. This is good enough. We'll let the matter rest if B stays this way. But if he goes back to his old ways, I'll have to bother you again with the job of bringing him back here and telling him that Tien doesn't accept his apologies."

The lieutenant colonel in the district police department had austere features. He was approaching retirement age.

"I hope it's over and done with," said the lieutenant colonel, still holding Thanh's hand. "I'm retiring next year. My wife and I have been going to Buddhist temples these past few years. My mind isn't as sharp as it used to be. I'm getting old."

Then he laughed out loud and gave Thanh a pat on the shoulder. Whether the lieutenant colonel felt happy or sad at that moment was unclear.

★★★

The whole flock of chickens kept running around at B's feet. The old hens were the boldest; the chicks weren't afraid of him either; only the ones in between appeared to be shy. As for the rooster, it would fastidiously pick up a grain of rice and then drop it and keep clucking for a member of his flock to come and eat it.

It turned out that B was good at raising chickens and his neighbors all praised him for his natural skills. In the beginning, he only had a rooster and two hens, and now, half a year later, he had this whole flock. Every time Mrs. B came to visit and brought him his pension, she would have dozens of eggs and one or two chickens to bring back to the city – a source of good food for herself and her daughter.

Every day, B enjoyed observing his chickens busily searching for food at the edge of the pond or the field, and in the garden. They kept scratching around in the soil for bits of food, and for B, it was so lively a scene and really fun to look at. B also kept a black dog of a tiny breed, but it was loyal and smart. It kept looking at him. When he sat down, deep in thought, it would lie down next to him. The moment he put on his shoes, it would jump up and go to the front door, waiting to go out with him. In the daytime, the countryside looked deserted. The young people had gone to school or to work in the city. Only their younger siblings and parents stayed behind. Then the younger siblings went to local schools while the parents went to toil in the fields or to do odd jobs around the village. Only a few elders could be seen watching their homes and taking care of their poultry. A world away from city life; here there was no cacophony of voices talking together and revving engines. There were only the sounds of birds in the trees and chickens on the ground, and of dogs on porches occasionally barking to chase away some chickens bold enough to try sneaking into a home for fun. There were no computers and there was no Internet. No newspapers. Only some news every now and then about current events on television --- soulless news items, invariably neutral and dull. At first, B wished he could talk with someone and could stay informed of events around the country. Gradually, he got used to his new life, and he began to be able to recognize the sound of each type of bird warbling in the eudicot or the carambola tree in the garden.

★★★

That day, when B came back from the district office, he had told Mr. Tu about how Tien had sued him for filing false charges against him. He told Mr. Tu about how he had had to plead for Tien's forgiveness. Mr. Tu had looked at everything critically and concluded that the case was not closed yet, and that things had only been temporarily set aside. You never knew when the other party would refuse to be reconciled and would press ahead with the lawsuit and drag you to court. Certainly, this kind of misdemeanor wouldn't lead to imprisonment, but B would have to see the cops many times before he would be brought to court. Then his wife would not know peace and his daughter could not concentrate on her studies.

The two of them had had a long conversation about all the details of the case, and they both had come to the conclusion that B should live in the countryside for a while, so that Tien would forget about him and not sue him. Then his daughter would feel secure enough to focus on her college entrance exams, and his wife could avoid being gossiped about at her school. Mrs. B only needed to teach a few more years before she could retire. But for the time being, she still had to stay employed and their daughter needed to finish school. Alone at home, Mr. Tu said, you never knew what might happen to you. If B stepped out of the house, he would run into belligerent neighbors. Even if he stayed inside his home, he would have to put up with the smoke from Mrs. Chinh's stove. Besides, there would be a few guys keeping his house under surveillance and taking pictures of his visitors and bothering them. There were a lot rumors going around that B was a reactionary, that he was being tailed, and that he was about to be arrested, which made everyone steer clear of him. But if he went and lived in the countryside, far away from everything, then the whole matter would soon blow over.

It was true that, ever since he came down here, Mrs. B had become much happier on her visits. She also said that her neighbors, when looking at the chickens she brought back with her, would compliment B on his natural talent for raising healthy chickens. They even wanted to buy his eggs and his chickens, knowing that being a kind person, his chickens would be free from the growth-promoting antibiotics normally fed to the chickens sold by greedy and unfeeling merchants in the market.

A year had gone by peacefully. From time to time, B would go back to the city to buy some things and stay at home for a day and then go back to the countryside right away because he needed to feed his poultry. His daughter had passed the entrance exam and was now attending the University of Education and would follow in her mother's footsteps. Thanks to the fact that her mother had taught for many years and been cited for many achievements, the school would offer her a teaching position following her graduation, which would be about the time when Mrs. B was ready to retire. Envisioning a future of family stability, each time when he was leaving the city and going past the flower garden in front of the Prime Minister's palace, B would bend his head, not daring to look at those skinny, wretched souls unfolding their straw mats on the sidewalk to lie down, lamenting and protesting about the loss of their land.

B was not the only one who bent his head. There were bloggers like him who had chosen to turn a blind eye to injustices suffered by the little people. There were those who wrote about the truth and then edited it many times until the truth became formless. The ones who had retired and were free like B had to put up with such sinister tricks. Then what about those who still had a job and faced so many family issues? They would have to bow their heads even lower. Although this country was small, the number of journalists and bloggers who were jailed was not small at all. And naturally, the number of truths which would not see the light of day was not small either.

Each person who wrote about the truth would have to consider the price they would have to pay, and each time they did that, the truth grew smaller.

★★★

Tien stepped into Thanh's office and saw him closing the file on Tran Van B.

"We are done with him, right?" asked Tien. "Damn the old guy! I haven't tried every trick in the book yet. I was planning to toss some feces into his house for him to enjoy the smell."

Thanh glared at him.

"You're talking nonsense. Police officers don't do dirty things like that. This kind of talk will disgrace the whole department. If you don't think of yourself, then think of your old man. He's about to become a general. Go verify the demonstration happening the other day, out there in front of the monument."

Tien handed him a list of expenses and snickered shamelessly.

"Please approve this so that I can go happily with some dough in my pocket."

★★★

Thanh's house had been built, and his daughter had abandoned the plan to major in administrative studies. Heeding his advice, she would take an exam to get into the police field.

Thanh said that in this field there would be no lack of administrative jobs, and when she took the exam, she would have priority over the other candidates because her father was in the police force. It would be easy to pass the exam and easy to find a job, he kept telling her. Eventually, she agreed after Thanh had promised that on graduation she would get an administrative position in the police department of the district where they lived. Her mother was doing good business.

Thanh smiled and thought that he should talk his wife into having another child. At her age, she could still bear another one, but in a few more years it would no longer be possible.

A solid family situation was an important factor in getting promoted to a leadership position. He lit a cigarette and blew the smoke out dreamily. Once B's case had been wrapped up nicely, surely the next time he would be promoted.

"Ah!" he exclaimed suddenly and reached for his phone and keyed in a phone number.

"Mr. Tu? If you're free this afternoon, I'd like to invite you to go out and have a drink with me after work. I've been too busy to stop by your house, and so I haven't had a chance to thank you for having advised your friend to do the right thing. Your help has saved us a lot of work."

At the other end, Mr. Tu declined the invitation as he was busy this afternoon. He hung up the phone and cursed Thanh.

"I did it for my friend, not for them. In this life, when you cannot fight against them, you have to save yourself. One day, they will reap what they have sown."

Having sent Tran Van B's file to his superior officers for their inspection, Thanh sat in his office, leaning back in his chair. Inside his head, he saw them one by one, a suspect by the name of C, another one by the name of A. They were much harder to deal with than B. They had connection with the reactionaries overseas. They were tenacious and cunning. These days, they were collaborating tightly with evicted citizens and religious groups. It was reported that they now openly contacted each other and gathered together. In addition, dissatisfied intellectuals were also getting involved, complicating the situation further.

Before his superiors handed out policies on how to deal with them, he would send his own agents to infiltrate their organizations, and then to obtain more information and to sow dissension within their ranks. But he would wait to hear from his superiors first, it wouldn't do to put the cart before the horse. In the meantime, it was best to just place a mole in their ranks. When there was an order from above, he would be ready. Thanh opened the file cabinet and pulled out a new folder and carefully penned a code name on it.

Berlin, December 25th, 2013